God or Religion:
The Truth

by Charles O. Young, Ph.D.

Printed in the United States of America
ISBN 978-0615489858

Contents

4

Prologue

To look at something as though we had never seen it before requires great courage. – Henri Matisse

In 1970, after having been a passive believer for 13 years, God moved in my life and led me to become a more overt Christian. I began sharing my faith. I vividly remember the night that God put it into my heart to change my focus from temporal things to things that last forever. While working in county government as a computer systems analyst, I was tasked with the oversight of the county payroll system. My responsibility included being present while the computer printed the bi-weekly paychecks. After a short few weeks or months watching the paychecks print, the thought crossed my mind that surely this isn't all there is to life. Life must be more than working for two weeks to get a paycheck, then working for two more weeks to get another and another and another, all the while spending every dime of it and more, creating nearly oppressive debt.

As I leaned on the printer that night, watching the checks print, a Bible passage crossed my mind, speaking to my heart in such a way that it moved me to action. The verses are found in I John 2:15, 16, and 17.

[15] Do not love the world or the things in the world. If anyone loves the world, the love of the Father is not in him. [16] For all that is in the world—the lust of the flesh, the lust of the eyes, and the pride of life—is not of the Father but is of the world. [17] And the world is passing away, and the lust of it; but he who does the will of God abides forever.

My mind began to process the words "pass away" and "forever." It occurred to me that during the vast majority of my life, thought processes and plans were focused on that which **passed away**. That night I realized that my priorities must be changed with more attention to that which lasts **forever**.

As I made adjustments in my life, the spiritual world began to come to the forefront, and I became interested in the spiritual lives of others. It cannot be denied that life is far more fulfilling as we lose sight of self and include "others" in our thought processes. I began to engage people inquiring about their spiritual lives. Surprisingly enough, I found that people are perfectly willing to share where they are on their spiritual journey, if they are not engaged in a threatening or condescending way.

It didn't take long for religion to become a topic of discussion. It turned out that most people are totally focused on religion, whether in a good way or bad, instead of being focused on God, because most equate being spiritual with being religious. In fact, as soon as religion comes up, people often become defensive. A lot of energy is spent defending one's religion, even if they do not practice it. Most peoples' religion comes from their upbringing, and it was never a clear choice that they made themselves. Someone once said, "You cannot reason a person out of a position that they did not reason themselves into." I have concluded that most atheists don't have as much argument with the idea of God as they do the idea of religion. They abhor mindless religion, and I think it's the mindlessness they protest, not the theology.

Years ago, I was speaking to a man who told me that he was an atheist. Actually, he was trying to give me a hard time and frustrate me a bit. I put my hand on his shoulder and closed my eyes and began to pray aloud, "Dear God, please strike this man dead right here in front of me. Make him fall down at my feet." The man knocked my hand off of his shoulder and jumped back, hollering, "What? Are you nuts?" I replied, "So you're not an atheist after all." Was he an atheist or just fed up with blind "faith" religion?

I believe religion is a set of *man-made* ideas, doctrines, rituals, practices, and dogmas. Even though some of those ideas may be correct, such as the existence of God, the theologies wrapped around those correct ideas dilute their truths. Theology itself, (the study of God) is an imperfect practice. In actuality, theology is whatever I *say* it is. Doctrine has become that which proves *my* religion. I may include the study of totem poles in *my* theology. It all has to do with *my* perspective.

In the little Book of Jude we see a vivid description of religion:

> *8 Likewise also these dreamers defile the flesh, reject authority, and speak evil of dignitaries. 9 Yet Michael the archangel, in contending with the devil, when he disputed about the body of Moses, dared not bring against him a reviling accusation, but said, "The Lord rebuke you!" 10 But these speak evil of whatever they do not know; and whatever they know naturally, like brute beasts, in these things they corrupt themselves. 11 Woe to them! For they have gone in the way of Cain, have run greedily in the error of Balaam for profit, and perished in the rebellion of Korah. 12 These are spots in your love feasts, while they feast with you without fear, serving only themselves. They are clouds without water, carried about[c] by the winds; late autumn trees without fruit, twice dead, pulled up by the roots; 13 raging waves of the sea, foaming up their own shame; wandering stars for whom is reserved the blackness of darkness forever.*

The "way of Cain" and "error of Balaam" and "rebellion of Korah" are really man-made religious ideas that have no spiritual substance. In fact, in verse 12 they are called "clouds without water." Can you imagine such a thing? It's an oxymoron!

Imagine the uselessness of a cloud that can not produce life-giving rain. Imagine religion that cannot connect with God.

In my quest to approach people on the spiritual level, religion has become my enemy. I find it to be a barrier between man and God. We know that the world is full of religion, and we also know that the world is not a very spiritual place.

This has become my view of religion, and in this book I will attempt to justify that view.

The Origin of Religion

Perfection is achieved not when there is nothing more to add, but when there is nothing left to take away. – Antoine de Saint Exupery

Before we can search for the origin of religion, we must first try to understand the meaning of the word 'religion'. We already have a complicated matter in that there are many twists to the word and its etymology. A generally-accepted definition is derived from two Latin words joined together, *re* (again) + *ligare* (to connect) or "to reconnect," *re-ligare*. The definition thus denotes an attempt by man to reconnect with God. Since man is trying to reconnect with God, the implication is that man perceives a "disconnect" with God. Since a disconnect is perceived, we can, therefore, deduce that religion is man's attempt to reconnect to God, making religion a **man-made** set of ideas, dogmas, doctrines, rituals, beliefs and practices to achieve the desired end: connection with God.

Wikipedia offers a definition that probably fits the worldview of most people, and so I will use Internet definitions throughout this book. These definitions do not reflect my own worldview, but they do create the contrast necessary to demonstrate the purpose of this writing.

Religion is the belief in and worship of a god or gods, or a set of beliefs concerning the origin and purpose of the universe. It is often described as communal belief in a supernatural, sacred or divine being. Many religions have narratives, symbols, traditions and sacred histories associated with their deity or deities, that are intended to give meaning to life. They tend to derive morality, ethics, religious laws or a preferred lifestyle from their ideas about the cosmos and human nature.

The word religion is sometimes used interchangeably with faith or belief system, but it is more than private belief and has a public aspect. Most religions have organized behaviors, congregations for prayer, priestly hierarchies, holy places and scriptures.

The development of religion has taken different forms in different cultures. Some religions place greater emphasis on belief, some on practice. Some emphasize the subjective experience of the religious individual, some the activities of the community. Some religions are universalistic, intending their claims to be binding on everyone; some are ethnic, intended only for one group. Religion often makes use of meditation, music and art. In many places it has been associated with public institutions such as education and the family and with government and political power.

Several ideas leap out to me from the above narrative:

1. God is implied, but seemingly not clearly defined; neither is God necessary to have a religion.

2. Multiple religions exist which demonstrate varied opinions of how to reach God.

3. Lifestyle and moral issues can be included which may improve ethnic relational behavior.

4. Cultural differences may dictate the form which a religion takes.

5. Individual beliefs exist which may, or may not, adhere to the general "religious" beliefs of the group.

6. The definition opens the door to a myriad of religions, perhaps as many as we have people.

7. Each religion may, in fact, have elements of truth, but not necessarily.

8. The above description allows for more than one God. By definition, God cannot have a peer; there can only be one supreme power. To even have subservient Gods would require a name change. He could not be called "God."

14

This author has studied religion and the Bible for more than 50 years, and has settled on six basic principles.

1. A cosmic struggle exists between God and Satan, good and evil

2. Religion is a barrier between man and God.

3. Religion is man-made, with most having a certain amount of truth.

4. "Truth" is found in the Bible..

5. Many religionists filter the Bible through their beliefs, and not the other way around.

6. The Bible is not a book of religion, it is God's Word.

Did religion start in Genesis 4?

> ", Now Adam knew Eve his wife, and she conceived and bore Cain, and said, "I have acquired a man from the LORD." , Then she bore again, this time his brother Abel. Now Abel was a keeper of sheep, but Cain was a tiller of the ground. , And in the process of time it came to pass that Cain brought an offering of the fruit of the ground to the LORD. , Abel also brought of the firstborn of his flock and of their fat. And the LORD respected Abel and his offering, , but He did not respect Cain and his offering. And Cain was very angry, and his countenance fell."

The Book of Genesis is a book of beginnings. Things recorded there are generally the first occurrences of those events. After Adam and Eve took their giant step away from God (the Fall) in Genesis 3, the next thing that we see in Genesis 4 is Cain and Abel acknowledging God by offering sacrifices. The very first notion of a sacrifice is found in the actions of God just after the Fall.

> *Genesis 3:21 "Also for Adam and his wife the LORD God made tunics of skin, and clothed them."*

God provided tunics or coats of skin to cover Adam's and Eve's newly-discovered nakedness. Where did God get this skin? Death had not entered the world until this experience, so God must have sacrificed an animal in order to make such a provision. We also know that Abel's method of sacrifice was an act of faith.

> *Hebrews 11:4 "By faith Abel offered to God a more excellent sacrifice than Cain…"*

Romans 10:17 tells us how faith is born:

> *"So then faith comes by hearing, and hearing by the word of God."*

We must, therefore, assume that Cain and Abel had prior instruction regarding making sacrifices.

16

A *blood* sacrifice is required by God (more on that later). Abel's sacrifice was accepted by God, but Cain's was rejected. Perhaps Cain chose his own sacrifice because it made sense to him that the sacrifice offered (fruit), being the result of his hard work, was a good thing. God gave him the chance to make it right, but Cain's pride was injured, and he chose to feed his anger instead of following God's way. Was this the beginning of religion? It should be noted here that God did not make allowance for Cain's good intentions. Cain's religion did not help him "reconnect" with God.

What was the purpose of the Tower of Babel?

> *Genesis 11: ", Now the whole earth had one language and one speech. , And it came to pass, as they journeyed from the east, that they found a plain in the land of Shinar, and they dwelt there. , Then they said to one another, "Come, let us make bricks and bake them thoroughly." They had brick for stone, and they had asphalt for mortar. , And they said, "Come, let us build ourselves a city, and a tower whose top is in the heavens; let us make a name for ourselves, lest we be scattered abroad over the face of the whole earth." , But the LORD came down to see the city and the tower which the sons of men had built. , And the LORD said, "Indeed the people are one and they all have one language, and this is what they begin to do; now nothing that they propose to do will be withheld from*

them. · Come, let Us go down and there confuse their language, that they may not understand one another's speech." · So the LORD scattered them abroad from there over the face of all the earth, and they ceased building the city. · Therefore its name is called Babel, because there the LORD confused the language of all the earth; and from there the LORD scattered them abroad over the face of all the earth."

I wonder why they wanted to reach into the heavens. Who or what did they think was there, although it seems that they certainly understood that God was there. In those early days, first-hand knowledge existed (Adam and Eve); they knew about God. It would seem that the inhabitants of Babel (later called Babylon, which is in modern Iraq) wanted to feed their own egos and exalt themselves, even to heaven, maybe to become Gods themselves. If you know anything about Satan, it sounds just like him.

Isaiah 14:13-14 "₁₃ For you(Satan) have said in your heart: ' I will ascend into heaven, I will exalt my throne above the stars of God; I will also sit on the mount of the congregation On the farthest sides of the north; I will ascend above the heights of the clouds, I will be like the Most High.'"

18

God had other ideas. If their attempts were to reach heaven, their attempts failed. Once again, man-made attempts (religion) failed to reconnect with God and His domain.

Why did Abraham build an altar?

> *Genesis 12: " Now the LORD had said to Abram: "Get out of your country, From your family And from your father's house, To a land that I will show you ₂ I will make you a great nation; I will bless you And make your name great; And you shall be a blessing. ₃ I will bless those who bless you, And I will curse him who curses you; And in you all the families of the earth shall be blessed." ₄ So Abram departed as the LORD had spoken to him, and Lot went with him. And Abram was seventy-five years old when he departed from Haran. ₅ Then Abram took Sarai his wife and Lot his brother's son, and all their possessions that they had gathered, and the people whom they had acquired in Haran, and they departed to go to the land of Canaan. So they came to the land of Canaan. ₆ Abram passed through the land to the place of Shechem, as far as the terebinth tree of Moreh.₍₆₎ And the Canaanites were then in the land. ₇ Then the LORD appeared to Abram and said, "To your descendants I will give this land." And there he built an altar to the LORD, who had appeared to him."*

After the world became corrupted by man's attempts to exalt himself, God chose a man named Abraham to begin a new ethnic group of people with whom He could entrust spiritual truths. He would commission Abraham and his descendants to be the custodians of the truths of God. Religion was to be discarded to allow truth to work in the hearts of man. God made promises to Abraham and to his descendants as He empowered them to share this good news of how God wanted to reach man. It will always be God reaching man, and not the other way around. My question has to do with the altar mentioned in Genesis 12:7: Did God instruct Abraham to build an altar? Was it a practice that he learned from his forefathers? Perhaps he invented the tradition himself. If so, Abraham or someone else before him instituted an interesting ceremony that would later be endorsed by God as He gave a 'blueprint' for tabernacle worship, fulfilled by His servant, Moses. It is a good practice to ask these questions about all religious ceremonies. Did they come from God or man?

What's up with Melchizedek?

> *Genesis 14: "₁₈ Then Melchizedek king of Salem brought out bread and wine; he was the priest of God Most High. ₁₉ And he blessed him and said: "Blessed be Abram of God Most High, Possessor of heaven and earth; ₂₀ And blessed be God Most High, Who has delivered your enemies into your hand." And he (Abraham) gave him a tithe of all."*

A new person was introduced to the world through this exchange. Abraham had just returned from a battle to protect his nephew, Lot, from the attack of local powers. Melchizedek approached Abraham and reminded him Who it was that had blessed him and delivered him from the trouble at hand. It was God!

But who is Melchizedek? He is called "king of Salem" and "the priest of God Most High." Suddenly we have a concept being added to our relationship experience with God, a priest. A priest is one who serves as a mediator between men and God. God will later instruct Moses as to the office of a priest, but that will not occur for some 700 years. There was no priesthood, no Mosaic law, and no such practice as a mediator. But here we have Melchizedek, as priest. Let's make this clear--God's Word is advocating a priest. In fact, this priest is a pre-law, pre-ceremony, pre-view of God's program for reaching man. Later, in the New Testament, we have an explanation of this person.

> *Hebrews 7: " For this Melchizedek, king of Salem, priest of the Most High God, who met Abraham returning from the slaughter of the kings and blessed him, ² to whom also Abraham gave a tenth part of all, first being translated "king of righteousness," and then also king of Salem, meaning "king of peace," ³ without father, without mother, without genealogy, having neither beginning of days nor end of life, but made like the Son of God, remains a priest continually."*

Who is this person who is called King of Peace? Who is this person without father and without mother, without descendants? Who is this King of Righteousness? Who has no beginning or end of life, and remains a priest continually? It is the Son of God! In God's program of reaching down to man, He injected His own Son into the world as a priest, a mediator, the link between Himself and man.

> *John 14:6 Jesus said to him, "I am the way, the truth, and the life. No one comes to the Father except through Me."*

> *I Timothy 2:5 "For there is one God and one Mediator between God and men, the Man Christ Jesus"*

> *Hebrews 4:14 "Seeing then that we have a great High Priest who has passed through the heavens, Jesus the Son of God, let us hold fast our confession. ¹⁵ For we do not have a High Priest who cannot sympathize with our weaknesses, but was in all points tempted as we are, yet without sin. ¹⁶ Let us therefore come boldly to the throne of grace that we may obtain mercy and find grace to help in time of need."*

> *I Peter 2: "Christ also suffered for us, leaving us an example, that you should follow His steps: ²² " Who committed no sin, Nor was deceit found in His mouth"; ²³ who, when He was reviled, did not revile in return; when*

*He suffered, He did not threaten, but committed Himself
to Him who judges righteously; ⁺ who Himself bore our
sins in His own body on the tree, that we, having died to
sins, might live for righteousness—by whose stripes you
were healed."*

Now we have two Biblical ideas converging: a sacrifice and a
priest. Guess what? Both of them are Jesus. This is **God's** plan,
not **man's** religion.

Abraham got it!

*Genesis 14:22: "But Abram said to the king of Sodom, "I
have raised my hand to the LORD, God Most High, the
Possessor of heaven and earth...."*

This is a very powerful confession coming from Abraham. He
acknowledged the authority and sovereignty of God, and
recognized that God is owner of all, including himself, Abraham.
This is true, simple, unadulterated worship, uncomplicated by the
shackles of man-made religion. There were no buildings, no holy
places, no rituals, no dogmas, no prohibition lists, no religious
garb, no ceremony, no holier-than-thou people. Just Abraham
coming to grips with his cosmic position in the universe, a mere
mortal in the presence of God, the creator of the universe.

*Genesis 15:6 "And he (Abraham) believed in the LORD,
and He (God) accounted it to him for righteousness."*

No religion here, just simple child-like faith, a relationship between Abraham and God.

Is religion synonymous with spirituality?

Our friends at Wikipedia have a definition of spirituality that is probably in the ballpark of most people:

> *Spirituality can refer to an ultimate or immaterial reality; an inner path enabling a person to discover the essence of their being; or the "deepest values and meanings by which people live." Spiritual practices, including meditation, prayer and contemplation, are intended to develop an individual's inner life; such practices often lead to an experience of connectedness with a larger reality, yielding a more comprehensive self; with other individuals or the human community; with nature or the cosmos; or with the divine realm. Spirituality is often experienced as a source of inspiration or orientation in life. It can encompass belief in immaterial realities or experiences of the immanent or transcendent nature of the world.*

This does not sound like the connection that Abraham had with God. Even though many people in the world would embrace the

24

notions of "spirituality," they do not yield to the superiority of God, or attempt to build a relationship with Him. These practices must surely leave a void of peace or fulfillment in a person's life. They are "clouds without water."

It is not in man's best interest to invent ideas that replace the need for God or ignore God's ways for man. Most religionists claim that they alone have found the way to God, and all others are wrong, missing the mark. With so many religions in the world claiming exclusivity, it is no wonder that people who seek true spiritual fulfillment are overwhelmed. In fact, if I were Satan, and I wanted to keep people from finding a true relationship with God, I would fill the world with religion.

The Development of Religion

Everything happening, great and small is a parable whereby God speaks to us. The art of life is to get the message. *-- Malcolm Muggeridge*

The worship and devotion to God that we see in the early parts of the Bible had nothing to do with religion. Since we have developed the idea that religion is man-made, and that God is inclined to reach down to man, the interaction with God that we see early on was not only approved by God, but also initiated by God.

While serving as a missionary in Portugal, I encountered a girl who I deemed to be a seeker. She admitted that she thought that there "was something there," but had not concluded that it was God. I asked her if she was opposed to calling the "something" God, and she seemed to have some reluctance. I told her I had an idea that she might try to put God to the test, so I suggested to her that she might pray that if God were real to please show up in her life. A week or so later I asked her if she had prayed that prayer. She acknowledged that she had but, so far, nothing had happened to make her believe in God. As we sat at the kitchen table, I leaned forward and said, "Nothing?" She said, "Nothing." I then told her to look across the table at me. "Do you know who I am?" I asked. "I am the messenger of God. God knew that you had questions and sent me 5,000 miles to help you understand and answer your questions." She told me that she hadn't thought of anything like that. From that experience, I recognized that most people wouldn't even know that God was trying to reach them. Most people want some miraculous event like handwriting on the wall or in the sky. They want more than a "chance encounter".

It is my considered opinion, based on experience, that God has a myriad of ways to reach down to us. It may be a health issue, or relationship failure, or a financial reversal that God uses to get our attention. I believe that God designed life so that, sooner or later, we would need Him. Often man has to find himself "way down" before he will look up--to God. It is always God reaching down to man.

Abraham heard directly from God.

> *Genesis 12:* ¹ *Now the LORD had said to Abram: "Get out of your country, From your family And from your father's house, To a land that I will show you.*
> ² *I will make you a great nation; I will bless you And make your name great; And you shall be a blessing. I will bless those who bless you, And I will curse him who curses you; And in you all the families of the earth shall be blessed."*

In the previous chapter, we introduced Abraham (2100 BC) as a person chosen by God to begin a new ethnic group of people. His instructions from God were to settle a new land, carrying the message of God to all the people of the world. At this point in Genesis 12, no "religion" existed in this pure relationship experience between Abraham and God.

Aaron became the first priest.

> *Exodus 28:* ¹ *"Now take Aaron your brother, and his sons with him, from among the children of Israel, that he may minister to Me as priest, Aaron and Aaron's sons: Nadab, Abihu, Elemazar, and Ithamar.* ² *And you shall make holy garments for Aaron your brother, for glory and for beauty.* ³ *So you shall speak to all who are gifted artisans, whom I have filled with the spirit of wisdom, that they may make Aaron's garments, to consecrate him, that he may minister to Me as priest.*

Seven hundred years after Abraham, Aaron became the first priest. I must resist the urge to discuss the Biblical history of the 700-year gap here. For the purposes of this writing, suffice it to say that it included the years of the patriarchs--Abraham, Isaac, Jacob (whose name was changed to Israel, thus producing descendants called the children of Israel or, simply, Israel), Joseph, and now Moses and his brother, Aaron. Moses (1440 BC) received the law from God after he led the children of Israel out of captivity from Egypt. This law included areas affecting the civil, dietary, moral, ceremonial, and spiritual parts of the lives of the descendants of Jacob or, from here on, Israel.

A part of the ceremonial law included the idea of a priest. Since we have already introduced Melchizedek as the priest of the most high God, Aaron will only be a representation or a figure of the ultimate Priest, Jesus. Later I will clarify what this priesthood means, but, for now, just know that a magnificent plan is afoot. Also note that none of this came from man. All of it came from God. This is not "religion."

David spoke directly to God.

The Book of Psalms is mostly attributed to David (1000 BC), the second king of Israel. As a young man, David had an incredible sensitivity to and relationship with God. From his writings in the Book of Psalms, the reader can get a sense of David's devotion and worshipful attitude toward God. Many of the Psalms depict David praying to God, expressing his sincere heart in admiration, repentance, and even in prophetic proclamation.

As king of Israel, David was most often engaged in a war of sorts with the kings of the region. Don't be too impressed with the idea of a local king. For one to become a king only required a self-proclamation and a semblance of a following. For instance, the oldest city in the world, Jericho, only covered six acres of land. Nevertheless, it was called a city. Even though God blessed David and Israel in battle, He did not embrace the bloodshed. David was, therefore, prevented by God from the privilege of building the first temple to God. It was to be a meeting place between God and man for centuries to come. This temple would also figure into the ultimate plan of God in His "reaching" down to man (more on this later). In David's leading of Israel and his own personal worship of God, no "religion" entered into the interaction. It was all as directed by God.

Solomon's heart was turned away by religion.

After the death of David, he was succeeded by his son, Solomon, as king of Israel. Solomon was more of a politician than David, and he made treaties with the local kings of the region. In fact, part of his strategy was to marry the daughters of the local kings, thus preserving the peace in the region. The local kings were not likely to attack the nation of Israel because their own daughters lived there.

> *I Kings 3:1* ¹ *Now Solomon made a treaty with Pharaoh king of Egypt, and married Pharaoh's daughter; then he brought her to the City of David until he had finished building his own house, and the house of the LORD, and the wall all around Jerusalem.*

Solomon was a good son, and he followed the footsteps of his father, David, in his personal walk with God. He had a heart for God, and he had a great relationship with God at the personal level. However, with his new wives in his kingdom, Solomon allowed them to practice the "religions" in which they were raised. It soon became a spiritual stumbling block to him.

I Kings 3: ² *Meanwhile the people sacrificed at the high places, because there was no house built for the name of the LORD until those days.* ³ *And Solomon loved the LORD, walking in the statutes of his father David, except that he sacrificed and burned incense at the high places.*

As time went on, God blessed Solomon with a supernatural wisdom that would become known throughout the middle-eastern world. Solomon's heart was seriously devoted to God.

I Kings 3: ⁴*Now the king went to Gibeon to sacrifice there, for that was the great high place: Solomon offered a thousand burnt offerings on that altar.* ⁵ *At Gibeon the LORD appeared to Solomon in a dream by night; and God said, "Ask! What shall I give you?"* ⁶ *And Solomon said: "You have shown great mercy to Your servant David my father, because he walked before You in truth, in righteousness, and in uprightness of heart with You; You have continued this great kindness for him, and You have given him a son to sit on his throne, as it is this day.* ⁷ *Now, O LORD my God, You have made Your servant king instead of my father David, but I am a little child; I do not know how to go out or come in.* ⁸ *And Your servant is in the midst of Your people whom You have chosen, a great people, too numerous to be numbered or counted.* ⁹ *Therefore give to Your servant an understanding heart to judge Your people, that I may* *discern between good and evil. For who is able to judge this great people of Yours?"*

[10] The speech pleased the Lord, that Solomon had asked this thing. [11] Then God said to him: "Because you have asked this thing, and have not asked long life for yourself, nor have asked riches for yourself, nor have asked the life of your enemies, but have asked for yourself understanding to discern justice, [12] behold, I have done according to your words; see, I have given you a wise and understanding heart, so that there has not been anyone like you before you, nor shall any like you arise after you. [13] And I have also given you what you have not asked: both riches and honor, so that there shall not be anyone like you among the kings all your days. [14] So if you walk in My ways, to keep My statutes and My commandments, as your father David walked, then I will lengthen your days."

It appears that God was very pleased with Solomon and his devotion to Him. There was no "religion" in the encounters that Solomon had with God. However, in time, Solomon's heart was turned away by his many wives and the religions of his wives.

I Kings 11: [1] But King Solomon loved many foreign women, as well as the daughter of Pharaoh: women of the Moabites, Ammonites, Edomites, Sidonians, and Hittites— [2] from the nations of whom the LORD had said to the children of Israel, "You shall not intermarry with them, nor they with you. Surely they will turn away your hearts after their gods." Solomon clung to these in love. ³ *And he had seven hundred wives, princesses, and three hundred concubines; and his wives turned away his heart.* ⁴ *For it was so, when Solomon was old, that his wives turned his heart after other gods; and his heart was not loyal to the LORD his God, as was the heart of his father David.* ⁵ *For Solomon went after Ashtoreth the goddess of the Sidonians, and after Milcom the abomination of the Ammonites.* ⁶ *Solomon did evil in the sight of the LORD, and did not fully follow the LORD, as did his father David.* ⁷ *Then Solomon built a high place for Chemosh the abomination of Moab, on the hill that is east of Jerusalem, and for Molech the abomination of the people of Ammon.* ⁸ *And he did likewise for all his foreign wives, who burned incense and sacrificed to their gods.* ⁹ *So the LORD became angry with Solomon, because his heart had turned from the LORD God of Israel, who had appeared to him twice,* ¹⁰ *and had commanded him concerning this thing, that he should not go after other gods; but he did not keep what the LORD had commanded.*

This is a classic example of what happens when religion comes between God and man. The nations mentioned above are cultures that evolved from our first father and mother, Adam and Eve. As time went on, they built religion around their knowledge of God's existence. In all cases they created idols, and even stooped so low as to sacrifice their own children as blood sacrifices.

Religion does NOT please God, and God is not interested in how dedicated you are to your religion. The world is full of religion, and the story of Solomon should warn everyone against following it. Clearly, there are also cross-cultural experiences listed here, and God allows for differences in culture, as long as the culture does not drag you into its man-made religion, distracting from the truth of God. This story also demonstrates how truth can be deteriorated by time and other influences. This will certainly explain why early church models no longer exist. Religion is more of a slow leak than a blowout. Gradually the religion takes precedence over truth. In fact, religion always evolves BEYOND truth.

Solomon's son messed up politically.

During the life of Solomon, as he was deeply involved in building the Temple of God and his own house, the nation experienced 20 years of heavy taxation. The center of national worship was now soundly fixed in the land of Israel at the Temple of God, which was built in Jerusalem. Someone had to provide the goods, as well as the people, necessary to build two very extravagant buildings. The taxation of the people and goods became oppressive. At the death of Solomon, Rehoboam, his son, ascended the throne of power over the nation of Israel. By that time, the nation was several million strong and neatly divided into 12 tribes, the land known today as Israel.

Early during the reign of Rehoboam, he was approached by the elders of the land, led by a national figure named Jeroboam, asking for a little relief from the heavy taxes. The elders thought that it would endear Rehoboam to the people if he would only lighten up some.

> *I Kings 12:* ¹ *And Rehoboam went to Shechem, for all Israel had gone to Shechem to make him king.* ² *So it happened, when Jeroboam the son of Nebat heard it (he was still in Egypt, for he had fled from the presence of King Solomon and had been dwelling in Egypt),* ³ *that they sent and called him. Then Jeroboam and the whole assembly of Israel came and spoke to Rehoboam, saying,* ⁴ *"Your father made our yoke heavy; now therefore, lighten the burdensome service of your father, and his heavy yoke which he put on us, and we will serve you."* ⁵ *So he said to them, "Depart for three days, then come back to me." And the people departed.* ⁶ *Then King Rehoboam consulted the elders who stood before his father Solomon while he still lived, and he said, "How do you advise me to answer these people?"* ⁷ *And they spoke to him, saying, "If you will be a servant to these people today, and serve them, and answer them,*

and speak good words to them, then they will be your servants forever." ⁸ *But he rejected the advice which the elders had given him, and consulted the young men who had grown up with him, who stood before him.* ⁹ *And he said to them, "What advice do you give? How should we answer this people who have spoken to me, saying, 'Lighten the yoke which your father put on us'?"* ¹⁰ *Then the young men who had grown up with him spoke to him, saying, "Thus you should speak to this people who have spoken to you, saying, 'Your father made our yoke heavy, but you make it lighter on us'—thus you shall say to them: 'My little finger shall be thicker than my father's waist!* ¹¹ *And now, whereas my father put a heavy yoke on you, I will add to your yoke; my father chastised you with whips, but I will chastise you with scourges!'"*

Rehoboam accepted the advice of the younger people, and rejected the advice of Jeroboam and the elders who represented the masses of the people. The result of not listening to the people ultimately divided the nation. Jeroboam did a little politicking, and convinced the ten northern tribes to follow him, making him their king, while the two southern tribes remained with *their* king Rehoboam. All was well for a short time until Jeroboam recognized a spiritual problem with the newly sectioned-off northern kingdom. The people were very thoroughly entrenched in their spiritual practice of attending the temple as God had designed. The problem was that the temple was located in Jerusalem, which was in the southern kingdom under the rule of Rehoboam. Jeroboam had to decide how to handle this situation.

I Kings 12: 25 Then Jeroboam built Shechem in the mountains of Ephraim, and dwelt there. Also he went out from there and built Penuel. 26 And Jeroboam said in his heart, "Now the kingdom may return to the house of David: 27 If these people go up to offer sacrifices in the house of the LORD at Jerusalem, then the heart of this people will turn back to their lord, Rehoboam king of Judah, and they will kill me and go back to Rehoboam king of Judah."

Now it gets interesting.

Jeroboam decided to start his own religion.

I Kings 12: 25 Then Jeroboam built Shechem in the mountains of Ephraim, and dwelt there. Also he went out from there and built Penuel. 26 And Jeroboam said in his heart, "Now the kingdom may return to the house of David: 27 If these people go up to offer sacrifices in the house of the LORD at Jerusalem, then the heart of this people will turn back to their lord, Rehoboam king of Judah, and they will kill me and go back to Rehoboam king of Judah." 28 Therefore the king asked advice, made two calves of gold, and said to the people, "It is too much for you to go up to Jerusalem. Here are your gods, O Israel, which brought you up from the land of Egypt!" [29] *And he set up one in Bethel, and the other he put in Dan.* [30] *Now this thing became a sin, for the people went to worship before the one as far as Dan.* [31] *He made shrines*[a] *on the high places, and made priests from every class of people, who were not of the sons of Levi.* [32] *Jeroboam ordained a feast on the fifteenth day of the eighth month, like the feast that was in Judah, and offered sacrifices on the altar. So he did at Bethel, sacrificing to the calves that he had made. And at Bethel he installed the priests of the high places which he had made.* [33] *So he made offerings on the altar which he had made at Bethel on the fifteenth day of the eighth month, in the month which he had devised in his own heart. And he ordained a feast for the children of Israel, and offered sacrifices on the altar and burned incense.*

Here are the features worthy of note as Jeroboam began his venture.

1. He reasoned within himself what would be right for him, not the people.

2. He didn't care what the spiritual implications were. What would God think? He didn't care. He was unconcerned about how God would react to the people going astray.

3. The two calves of gold that were crafted were in the distant memory of the people, as some were made as idols during the exodus from Egypt, 400 years earlier. The people had some cloudy memory of "calves." Therefore, this seemed OK.

4. Jeroboam led the people into idolatry, which was in direct disobedience to God's commands.

5. He told a lie about the calves, and arbitrarily deified them.

6. The people were accustomed to feast days, so he created his own, and included them in his religion.

7. Sacrifices were also a part of his practices, and the people were accustomed to these as well.

8. The people paid spiritually for the offense, losing the blessing of God by violating the will of God.

This is how many religions start; i.e., for the benefit of a person or a group of people. Many or all of these steps are repeated over and over in the world as religions are developed to try to capture the heart and minds of people of the culture. One of the by-products of religion is that it can also be used to *control* the people.

A clear warning is given to us in the New Testament regarding the forming of religion. Ephesians 4 contains a narrative explaining that God has provided His word and the tools to help us understand that we should avoid such practices.

> *Ephesians 4: ₁₄ "that we should no longer be children, tossed to and fro and carried about with every wind of doctrine, by the trickery of men, in the cunning craftiness of deceitful plotting"*

The only way that we can succeed in not falling for the devices of men attempting to lead us astray is to have a good understanding of God and His way through His Word.

Religion is our enemy. Early believers like Abraham, Moses, Aaron, David and many others, were not encumbered by the heavy burdens that religion produces. Each individual has a responsibility to God and to himself not to fall into the trappings of religion, but to build a relationship with God at the personal level. Religion will make that relationship complicated at best, and impossible at worst.

Major Religions of the World

There have been men before now who got so interested in proving the existence of God that they came to care nothing for God Himself. -- C.S. Lewis

How many religions are there anyway? It has been said that there are 30,000 variations of the Christian religion alone. There are hundreds of other stated religions, each one with many variations, not to mention the idiosyncrasies of each person. This chapter will discuss the eight most prominent religions of the world, starting with Internet definitions, and they attempt to be all encompassing within the framework of the stated religion. As I read the definitions, I realize that they will probably offend people of each variation because of the attitudes of exclusivity and the denominational arrogance held by each group. When I was a missionary in Portugal, I was asked to which religion I belonged. I recognized that regardless of my answer, my spiritual state would not be understood. I said that I was Christian. The hearer interpreted that to mean I was old-world Catholic because that was his frame of reference. I quickly learned to say that I was a follower of Jesus. That, too, made me seem weird because I didn't espouse a "formal" religion. I finally concluded that religion itself was my enemy. It put up an instant barrier between me and the people I was trying to reach.

As you read the definitions, note the main features of each one. It will become apparent that each religion has its own divisions within it. You also may envision the evolution of each religion over time. Religion always evolves, and the differences within each religion have produced great violence over the history of the religion. Wars have been fought, people have been murdered or maimed, nations have been divided, and centuries of upheaval have been produced by the dogmatic variances found in each religion. For years, Ireland was engaged in civil war that existed because of the differences between Protestants and Catholics, both "Christian" religions. Can you imagine killing your fellow countrymen invoking the name of Christ? Pakistan would not exist today were it not for the differences between the Muslims and the Hindus of India. Hundreds of thousands of Indians were killed because of the differences between these two religions. Invoking the name of God, cousins killed each other in war. Surely this is not what God intended; this is religion at its worst.

Descriptions of the eight major religions follow; **they are taken directly from the Internet**. These quotes are not intended as an endorsement of the religions, and no further explanation will be included.

Major Religions of the World Ranked by Number of Adherents

1. **Christianity: 2.1 billion**

Overview of Christianity

With nearly two billion professed adherents worldwide, Christianity is currently the **largest religion in the world**. It has dominated western culture for centuries and remains the majority religion of Europe and the Americas. **Christian belief** centers on the life of **Jesus of Nazareth**, a teacher and healer of first-century Palestine. The primary source of information about the life of Jesus are the **Gospels**, four books written by different authors 30-100 years after Jesus' death. The Gospels eventually became the first four books of the **New Testament**.

The Gospels describe a three-year teaching and healing ministry during which Jesus attracted 12 close disciples and other followers who believed him to be the Messiah. This is the basis of Jesus' title "Christ," which comes from the Greek word for "Messiah." Jesus' teachings focused on the themes of the kingdom of God, love of God and love of neighbor. Along with some of his teachings, his growing popularity with the masses was seen as dangerous by Jewish religious leaders and the Roman government, leading to his execution by crucifixion. Christians believe Jesus rose from the dead three days after his burial, and in so doing made it possible for those who believe to be forgiven of sin and attain eternal life. Much of Christian belief and practice centers on the **resurrection of Christ**. The most distinctive belief of mainstream Christianity is the doctrine of the **Trinity**, which views the **one God** as consisting of three Persons: the Father, the Son (**Christ**) and the **Holy Spirit**.

The sacred text of Christianity is the **Bible**, which consists of the **Old Testament** (roughly equivalent to the Jewish Bible) and the **New**

Testament. The New Testament contains 27 books: **four gospels** (narratives of Jesus' life), one account of the apostles' ministry after Jesus' death, letters from church leaders (the earliest of which predate the Gospels), and an apocalyptic work. Nearly all Christians regard the Bible as divinely inspired and authoritative, but **views differ** as to the nature and extent of its authority. Some hold it to be completely without error in all matters it addresses, while others stress its accuracy only in religious matters and allow for errors or limitations in other areas due to its human authorship. Christianity has **divided** into three major branches over the centuries. **Roman Catholicism** represents the continuation of the historical organized church as it developed in Western Europe, and is headed by the Pope. Distinctive beliefs of Catholics include the doctrines of Transubstantiation and Purgatory, and distinctive practices include devotion to the saints and **Mary** and use of the rosary. **Eastern Orthodoxy** (which includes the Greek and Russian Orthodox Churches and several others) is the continuation of the historical organized church as it developed in Eastern Europe. It differs from Catholicism in its refusal of allegiance to the Pope, its emphasis on the use of icons in worship, and the date it celebrates Easter. Other cultural, political, and religious differences exist as well. Eastern Orthodoxy and Roman Catholicism separated in 1054 AD, when the Patriarch of Constantinople and the Pope excommunicated each other. **Protestantism** arose in the 16th century during the Reformation, which took place mainly in Germany, Switzerland, and Britain. Protestants do not acknowledge the authority of the Pope, reject many traditions and beliefs of the Catholic Church, emphasize the importance of reading the

Bible and hold to the doctrine of salvation by faith alone. Protestantism encompasses numerous denominational groups, including Lutherans, Baptists, Methodists, Episcopalians, Presbyterians, Pentecostals and Evangelicals. **Christian practices** vary by denomination, but common elements include a Sunday worship service, private and corporate prayer, study and reading of the Scriptures, and participation in rites such as baptism and communion. **Distinctive Catholic practices** include recognition of seven total sacraments, Sunday mass, devotion to the Virgin Mary and the saints, and veneration of relics and places associated with holy figures. Eastern Orthodoxy holds many practices in common with Catholicism, but is especially distinguished by the central role of icons: ornate images of Christ and the saints believed to provide a connection to the spiritual world.

2.   Islam: 1.5 billion

Islam is the 2nd largest religion in the world, with over 1 billion followers. It is a monotheistic faith founded by a man named Muhammad in 7th century Saudi Arabia.

According to Muslim belief, the angel Gabriel appeared to Muhammad, a camel driver, in a mountain cave and delivered a message from the one true God. The Prophet Muhammad dedicated the remainder of his life to spreading a message of monotheism in a polytheistic world. His life's work is recorded in the Qur'an, the sacred text of Islam. In 622 AD, the Prophet fled north to the city of Medina to escape growing persecution. This event is celebrated by Muslims as the *hijira* ("flight") and marks the beginning of the Islamic calendar (622 AD = 1 AH). Eight years later, Muhammad returned to Mecca with an army and defeated it easily. By Muhammad's death, 50 years later, the entire Arabian Peninsula had come under Muslim control. The word "Islam" means "submission," reflecting the religion's central tenet of submitting to the will of God. Islamic practices center on the Five Pillars of Islam: confession of faith, daily prayer, fasting during Ramadan, pilgrimage and charity. The sacred text of Islam, the Qur'an, was written in Arabic within 30 years of Muhammad's death. Muslims believe it contains the literal word of God as gradually revealed to Muhammad by the Angel Gabriel over the course of 20 years. Also important is the tradition of the sayings and actions of the Prophet and his Companions, collected in the hadith.

3.   **Secular – Nonreligious – Agnostic - Atheist:**

1.1 billion (taken directly from the Internet)

Our Mission

The Secular Web is owned and operated by Internet Infidels, Inc., a 501(c)(3) nonprofit educational organization dedicated to defending and promoting a naturalistic worldview on the Internet. Naturalism is the "hypothesis that the natural world is a closed system" in the sense that "nothing that is not a part of the natural world affects it." As such, "naturalism implies that there are no supernatural entities," such as gods, angels, demons, ghosts, or other spirits, "or at least none that actually exercises its power to affect the natural world." And without miraculous interventions into nature from a spiritual realm, neither prayer nor magic are more effective than a placebo.

Our Value to You

Since its founding in 1995, the Secular Web has grown from a small site spawned in a dorm at Texas A&M University into the most comprehensive free thought resource on the Internet. We offer thousands of outstanding essays, reviews, and critiques, covering everything from articles of general interest to scholarly papers by prominent non-theistic philosophers, scientists, historians, and others. Unlike most of our opponents, we even publish responses to our own pieces to encourage readers to make up their own minds. In addition to such encyclopedic resources, other features of the site are outlined in the Secular Web pamphlet, which readers may download, print out, and distribute, as desired.

Why You Should Care

Life is short. Nevertheless, billions of people invest incalculable hours making fruitless pleas to nonexistent gods, participating in lavish rituals with no tangible effects, and whittling away tight budgets to support extravagant religious institutions or "spiritual advisors." Worse still, antiquated religious ideas lead people to impose needless hardships on themselves and others, to rationalize discrimination and other forms of mistreatment, and to hasten environmental destruction because they believe that "the end of the world" is imminent anyway. And for every outward manifestation of wasteful, counterproductive, and even downright harmful activity motivated *only* by religious belief, there are countless instances that are not nearly so obvious. Religious belief has exacted a toll on people's emotional well-being as well. Just how much energy has been drained searching for meaning where none is to be found, or been squandered on false hopes and unwarranted fears? How many believers have agonized over the uncertain destination of their loved ones after death? How many have struggled to discern exactly what they did to displease God after falling victim to a natural disaster? How many have been tormented trying to make sense of why God allows terrible things to happen to good people? In the <u>absence of any clear revelation about what God wants us to do</u>, how many have fretted about whether their own actions or beliefs, or those of the people dearest to them, are enough to avoid hellfire? How many of those who have lost their faith in old age have looked back at all the missed opportunities, the roads not taken, the life that could have been, had they not been born in a religious household, or had they abandoned religion in their younger days! Imagine how deep the regrets must be for the <u>former missionary</u>, <u>seminary student</u>, or <u>long-time minister</u> after realizing that this life is probably the only life that one will ever have.

4. <u>Hinduism</u>: 900 million

Overview of Hinduism

About <u>80 percent of India's population</u> regard themselves as Hindus and 30 million more Hindus live outside of India. There are a total of 900 million Hindus worldwide, making Hinduism the 4th largest. The term

"Hinduism" includes numerous traditions, which are closely related and share common themes but do not constitute a unified set of beliefs or practices.

Hinduism is thought to have gotten its name from the Persian word *hindu*, meaning "river," used by outsiders to describe the people of the Indus River Valley. Hindus themselves refer to their religion as *sanatama dharma*, "eternal religion," and *varnasramadharma*, a word emphasizing the fulfillment of duties (*dharma*) appropriate to one's class (*varna*) and stage of life (*asrama*). Hinduism has no founder or date of origin. The authors and dates of most Hindu <u>sacred texts</u> are unknown. Scholars describe modern Hinduism as the product of religious development in India that spans nearly four thousand years, making it the oldest surviving world religion. Indeed, as seen above, Hindus regard their religion as eternal (*sanatama*). Hinduism is not a homogeneous, organized system. Many Hindus are devoted followers of Shiva or Vishnu, whom they regard as the only true God, while others look inward to the divine Self (*atman*). But most recognize the existence of Brahman, the unifying principle and Supreme Reality behind all that is.

Most Hindus respect the authority of the Vedas (a collection of ancient <u>sacred texts</u>) and the Brahmans (the priestly class), but some reject one of both of these authorities. Hindu religious life might take the form of devotion to <u>God or gods</u>, the duties of family life, or concentrated meditation. Given all this diversity, it is important to take care when generalizing about "Hinduism" or "Hindu beliefs." The first sacred writings of Hinduism, which date to about 1200 BC, were primarily concerned with the ritual sacrifices associated with numerous gods who represented forces of nature. A more philosophical focus began to develop around 700 BC, with the Upanishads and development of the Vedanta philosophy. Around 500 BC, several new belief systems sprouted from Hinduism, most significantly Buddhism and Jainism.

5. ## Chinese traditional religion: 394 million

Chinese religion is not an organized, unified system of beliefs and practices. It has no leadership, no headquarters, no founder, and no denominations. Instead, "Chinese religion" is a general term used to describe the complex interaction of different religious and philosophical traditions that have been especially influential in China. Although other religious traditions have been influential in China, Chinese religion is primarily composed of four main traditions: Chinese folk religion, Confucianism, Taoism and Buddhism. The religious outlook of most Chinese people consists of some combination of beliefs and practices from these four traditions. It is very rare for only one to be practiced to the exclusion of the others. Buddhism, Taoism, and Confucianism, each of which is a significant part of Chinese religion, are treated in their own sections on Religion Facts. This section focuses especially on Chinese folk or indigenous religion, but reference is also made to the other traditions.

6. ## Buddhism: 376 million

Buddhism was founded by an Indian prince named <u>Siddharta Gautama</u> around the year 500 BCE. According to tradition, the young prince lived an affluent and sheltered life until a journey during which he saw an old man, a sick man, a poor man, and a corpse. Shocked and distressed at the suffering in the world, Gautama left his family to seek enlightenment through asceticism. But even the most extreme asceticism failed to bring enlightenment.

Finally, Gautama sat beneath a tree and vowed not to move until he had attained enlightenment. Days later, he arose as the Buddha - the "enlightened one." He spent the remaining 45 years of his life teaching the path to liberation from suffering (the *dharma*) and establishing a community of monks (the *sangha*). Today, there are over <u>360 million followers</u> of Buddhism. Although virtually extinct in its birthplace of India, it is prevalent throughout China, Japan and Southeast Asia. In the 20th century, Buddhism expanded its influence to the West and even to western religions. There are now over one million American Buddhists and even a significant number of "Jewish Buddhists." Buddhist concepts have also been influential on western society in general, primarily in the areas of meditation and nonviolence. <u>Buddhist beliefs</u> vary significantly across various sects and schools, but all share an admiration for the figure of the Buddha and the goal of ending suffering and the cycle of rebirth. <u>Theravada Buddhism</u>, prominent in Southeast Asia, is atheistic and philosophical in nature and focuses on the monastic life and meditation as means to liberation. <u>Mahayana Buddhism</u>, prominent in China and Japan, incorporates several deities, celestial beings, and other traditional religious elements. In Mahayana, the path to liberation may include religious ritual, devotion, meditation, or a combination of these elements. Zen, Nichiren, Tendai, and Pure Land are the major forms of Mahayana Buddhism.

7.   **<u>Sikhism</u>: 23 million**

The word "Sikhism" derives from "Sikh," which means a strong and able disciple. There are about 23 million Sikhs worldwide, making Sikhism the 7th largest religion in the world. Approximately 19 million Sikhs live in India, primarily in the state of Punjab. Large populations of Sikhs can also be found in the United Kingdom, Canada, and the United States. Sikhs are a significant minority in Malaysia and Singapore, where they are sometimes ridiculed for their distinctive appearance, but respected for their work ethic and high education standards. Sikhism emerged in 16th-century India in an environment heavily permeated with conflicts between the Hindu and Muslim religions. It was somewhat influenced by reform movements in Hinduism (e.g. Bhakti, monism, Vedic metaphysics, guru ideal, and bhajans) as well as some Sufi Muslim influences. While Sikhism reflects its cultural context, it certainly developed into a movement unique in India. Sikhs regard their faith as an authentic new divine revelation. Sikhism was founded by Guru Nanak Dev, who was born in 1469 to a Hindu family. After four epic journeys (north to Tibet, south to Sri Lanka, east to Bengal and west to Mecca and Baghdad), Guru Nanak preached to Hindus, Muslims and others, and in the process attracted a following of Sikhs (disciples). Religion, he taught, was a way to unite people, but in practice he found that it set men against one another. He particularly regretted the antagonism between Hindus and Muslims. Guru Nanak's most famous saying is, "There is no Hindu, there is no Muslim, so whose path shall I follow? I shall follow the path of God." Retaining the Hindu doctrine of the transmigration of souls, together with its corollary, the law of karma, Guru Nanak advised his followers to end the cycle of reincarnation by living a disciplined life – that is, by moderating egoism and sensuous delights, to live in a balanced worldly manner, and by accepting ultimate reality. Thus, by the grace of Guru (Gurprasad) the cycle of reincarnation can be broken, and the Sikh can remain in the abode of the Love of God. Guru Nanak taught that salvation does not mean entering paradise after a last judgment, but a union and absorption into God, the True Name. Sikhs do not believe in a heaven or hell. Sikhs also reject the Hindu belief in incarnations (avatars) of God, believing instead that God makes his will know through the Gurus. The most easily observable Sikh practices are the wearing of the turban and the Five Ks. Sikhs also pray regularly and meditate by repeating God's name, often with the aid of rosary beads. Sikhism rejects the Hindu notion of the four stages of life, teaching instead that the householder is the ideal for all people. A Sikh aims to live a life that balances work, worship and charity. Community is emphasized, and the Sikh temple (gurdwara) is the center of Sikh communal life.

8.   ## Judaism: 14 million

The central religious belief of Judaism is that there is only one God. Monotheism was uncommon at the time Judaism was born, but according to Jewish tradition, God himself revealed it to Abraham, the ancestor of the Jewish people. Beginning with Abraham, God has always taken special care of the Hebrews (who would later become the Jews). After rescuing them from slavery in Egypt, God revealed the Ten Commandments to Moses, and many more religious and ethical guidelines in the Torah ("the Law"). Many of the guidelines (*mitzvah*) emphasized ritual purity and the importance of remaining set apart from the surrounding polytheistic cultures. Aside from its staunch monotheism, Judaism has few essential beliefs. Jewish identity arises primarily from belonging to an ancient people and upholding its traditions. Dogma, while important, is secondary. Although the medieval thinker Rabbi Maimonides once enumerated "13 Articles of Faith," many Jews do not accept all these, and Jewish beliefs vary widely on theological matters such as human nature and the afterlife. Divisions within Judaism, known as "movements," have developed in modern times as varying responses to secularism and modernity. Orthodox Judaism is the most conservative group, retaining nearly all traditional rituals and practices. At the opposite end of the spectrum, Reform Jews retain their Jewish identity and some traditions but take a liberal approach to many Jewish beliefs and practices. Conservative Judaism lies in the middle of the spectrum, taking a moderate approach in its application of Judaism to the modern world. Jews of all movement celebrate many special days throughout the year and throughout each person's life. Major religious holidays include Passover, Rosh Hashanah and Yom Kippur. Hanukkah, historically a minor holiday, has become more prominent in the last century for Jews who live in areas that celebrate Christmas. The Sabbath, a day of rest and worship at the synagogue, is observed each Saturday. In Judaism, all days begin at sunset, so all holidays begin at sundown and end at sundown.

Religion Evolving

Christendom has done away with Christianity without quite being aware of it. –Soren Kierkegaard

The message of Christ is not Christianity. The message of Christ is Christ. --Gary Amirault

There are things about organized religion which I resent. Christ is revered as the Prince of Peace, but more blood has been shed in His name than any other figure in history. You show me one step forward in the name of religion and I'll show you a hundred retrogressions. Remember, they were men of God who destroyed the educational treasures at Alexandria, who perpetrated the Inquisition in Spain, who burned the witches at Salem. Over 25,000 organized religions flourish on this planet, but the followers of each think all the others are miserably misguided and probably evil as well. – Frank Sinatra

Religion always evolves beyond truth. Most religion contains some truth even if it is only the acknowledgement that God exists. From there, people begin to build their own ideas into their culture-driven, self-interest-driven, ego-driven, perceived-need-driven practices. In chapter three, our example of Jeroboam building his own religion contains all of these elements (I Kings 12). He knew what practices the people of his culture were accustomed to performing. His own self-interest drove him to try to control the group by providing a "religious" outlet. His ego was well served in that he had the power to move the people and he used it. His need for self-preservation was a huge driving force in his creation and further development of the religion. Shamefully, he produced his religion with no thought for the spiritual well-being of the people.

Even though every group but one would resist the idea, the Catholic Church is the global driving force of Christianity. In the world media, it is referred to as "the church." Since "Christianity" is the largest "religion" in the world (2.1 billion), and Catholicism is by far the largest division or denomination of that group, we can single them out as an example of religion evolving. This example by no means excludes all of the other denominations. Each one has evolved in its own way and for its own purposes, beyond truth. It is, in fact, quite astonishing to hear each denomination justify its own existence. Jesus said in John 15:17 *"These things I command you, that you love one another."* In the largest religion in the world, Christianity, instead of following the teachings of Jesus to love one another, we have instead divided into groups that generally despise one another. Most of our spiritual energy is spent defending our "denomination." *We don't need to love one another, it seems, we have denominations instead.* We could just try killing everyone that doesn't believe the way we do. It has, in fact, been tried for centuries by inquisitions, holy wars, ethnic cleansing, crusades, purifications, holocausts, terrorist attacks and simple outright murder.

For the purpose of this example, we will take a look at the evolution of the Catholic Church for the reasons stated above. Below is a fairly comprehensive list of what has been dubbed "Roman Catholic Inventions." The list is an historic view of man building religion beyond truth, in most cases without even a hint of Scriptural justification. It is a very interesting study to examine each invention and research the reason for its genesis. If you are a Catholic, resist the urge to nitpick the list. I am not attacking Catholics. My purpose is to simply show that religion changes, and not to defend the use of the list.

Inventions by the Catholic Church

and the dates of their adoption over a period of 1,650 years.

Because terms may be unclear, explanations have been provided in the footnotes.

1. **Prayers for the dead** - 300

2. **Making the sign of the cross** - 300

3. **Wax candles** - *about* 320

4. **Veneration of angels and dead saints, and use of images** - 375

5. **The Mass**, as a daily celebration - 394

6. ***Beginning of the exaltation of Mary***, the term "Mother of God" first applied to her by the Council of Ephesus - 431

7. ***Priests began to dress differently from laymen*** - 500

8. ***Extreme Unction[1]*** - 526

9. **The doctrine of Purgatory**, established by Gregory I - 593

10. ***Latin Language***, used in prayer and worship, imposed by Gregory I – 600.

11. ***Prayers directed to Mary, dead saints and angels*** - about 600

12. ***Title of pope***, or universal bishop, given to Boniface III, by emperor Phocas - 607

13. ***Kissing of the pope's foot***, began with Pope Constantine - 709

14. ***Temporal[2] power of the popes***, conferred by Pipin, king of the Franks - 750

15. ***Worship of the cross, images, and relics*** - authorized 786

16. ***Holy water*** mixed with a pinch of salt and blessed by a priest - 850

17. ***Worship of St. Joseph*** - 890

18. ***College of cardinals*** - established 927

19. ***Baptism of bells***, instituted by Pope John XIII - 965

20. ***Canonization[3] of dead saints***, first by Pope John XV - 995

21. ***Fasting on Fridays and during lent*** - 998

62

22. *The Mass*, developed gradually as a sacrifice, attendance made

obligatory in the 11th century

23. *Celibacy of the priesthood*, decreed by Pope Gregory VII - 1079

24. *The Rosary*, mechanical praying with beads, invented by Peter the Hermit - 1090

25. *The Inquisition4*, instituted by the Council of Verona - 1184

26. *Sale of Indulgences5* (see definition below) - 1190

27. *Transubstantiation6*, proclaimed by Pope Innocent III - 1215

28. *Auricular (out loud) Confession of sins to a priest instead of to God*,

instituted by Pope Innocent III, in Lateral council - 1215

29. *Adoration7 of the wafer* (Host), decreed by Pope Honorius III 1220

30. *Bible forbidden to laymen*, placed on the Index of Forbidden Books

by the Council of Toulouse - 1229

31. *The Scapular8*, invented by Simon Stock, an English monk - 1251

32. *Cup forbidden to the people* at communion by Council of Constance - 1414

33. *Purgatory9* proclaimed as a dogma by the Council of Florence - 1439

34. *The doctrine of Seven Sacraments* affirmed - 1439

35. *The Ave Maria (Hail Mary)* (part of last half finished 50 years later) - 1508

36. *Jesuit order* founded by Loyola - 1534

37. *Tradition declared as equal authority with the Bible* /Council of Trent - 1545

38. *Apocryphal books[10] added* to the Bible by the Council of Trent - 1546

39. *Creed of Pope Pius IV* imposed as the official creed - 1560

40. *Immaculate Conception[11]* of the Virgin Mary, proclaimed by Pope Pius IX - 1854

41. *Syllabus of Errors*, proclaimed by Pope Pius IX, and ratified by the Vatican Council, condemned freedom of religion, conscience, speech, press, and scientific discoveries which are disapproved by the Roman Church, asserted the popes' temporal authority over all civil rulers. - 1864

42. *Infallibility of the pope[12]* in matters of faith and morals, proclaimed by the Vatican Council - 1870

43. *Public Schools condemned* by Pope Pius XI - 1930

44. *Assumption[13] of the Virgin Mary* (bodily ascension into heaven shortly after her death), proclaimed by Pope Pius XII - 1950

45. Mary proclaimed *Mother of the Church*, by Pope Paul VI - 1965

This list of Catholic Inventions compiled by:

Boettner, Loraine, *Roman Catholicism,* The Presbyterian and Reformed Publishing Company: Phillipsburg, 1962. Pg. 7-9.

Definitions/ Explanations in footnotes provided by:

1 **Extreme Unction** *"the sacrament of anointing the sick in the Rom. Cath. Ch."* (*Webster's Dictionary, p. 463*)

2 **Temporal** *"pertaining to the present life, worldly."* (*Webster's Dictionary, p. 1325*)

3 **Canonization** to declare (a dead person) officially as a saint. (*Webster's Dictionary, p. 193*)

4 **Inquisition** *"a formal special tribunal, engaged chiefly in combating and punishing heresy"* (*Webster's, p. 675*)

5 **Indulgences** *"a partial remission (by the Roman Church) of the temporal punishment that is still due for sin after absolution.* (*Webster's Dictionary, p. 666*)

6 **Transubstantiation** *"the changing of one substance into another. 2. (in the Eucharist) the conversion of the whole substance* of the bread and wine into the body and blood of Christ, only the appearance of bread and wine remaining. (*Webster's Dictionary, p. 1368*)

7 **Adoration** *"the act of paying honor, as to a divine being; worship"* (*Webster's Dictionary, p. 18*) Random House Webster's College Dictionary, Random House New York. 1996.

Catechism of the Catholic Church, Doubleday New York, 1995.

8 **The Scapular** *"either of two small cloth pieces joined by strings passing over the shoulders, worn under clothing* as a badge of affiliation with a religious order or as an act of religious devotion." (*Webster's Dictionary, p. 1156*)

9 **Purgatory** *"(esp. in Roman Catholic belief) a place or state following death in which penitent souls are purified of* venial sins or undergo the temporal punishment still remaining for forgiven mortal sins and thereby are made ready for heaven. 2. Any condition or place of temporary punishment, suffering, or expiation. (*Webster's, p. 1058*)

10 **Apocryphal books** *"1. A group of books not found in Jewish or Protestant versions of the Old Testament but*
included in the Septuagint and Roman Catholic editions of the Bible; 2. various religious writings of uncertain
origin; 3. Writings or statements of doubtful authenticity." (Webster's Dictionary, 62)

11 **Immaculate Conception** *"(Mary) was redeemed (given salvation) from the moment of her conception." (Catholic*
Catechism, article 491)

12 **Infallibility** *"immune from fallacy, or error in expounding matters of faith and morals." (Webster's Dictionary)*

13 **Assumption** *"Finally, the Immaculate Virgin, preserved free from all stain of original sin, when the course of her*
earthly life was finished, was taken up body and soul into heavenly glory..." (Catholic Catechism, article 491)
"(Mary) committed no sin of any kind during her whole earthly life" (Catholic Catechism, article 411)

The list provokes several questions from this author. Since a date is fixed on a specific invention, what was the effective change on the "religion?" For instance, since the Pope was declared infallible around 1870 AD (item 42), did infallibility exist prior to that time? Since there was no official "Pope" prior to 607 AD (item 12) and he was promoted by the Emperor of the time, did God recognize this position and insure his infallibility? Were there any politics involved in this promotion? Can this position be justified by Scripture? Since the Pope is deemed to be the highest of priests (mediator), does that violate the authority given only to Jesus?

I Timothy 2:5 "For there is one God and one Mediator between God and men, the Man Christ Jesus"

Hebrews 4: "[14] Seeing then that we have a great High Priest who has passed through the heavens, Jesus the Son of God, let us hold fast our confession. [15] For we do not have a High Priest who cannot sympathize with our weaknesses, but was in all points tempted as we are, yet without sin."

Since we are questioning "mediator" what about praying to Mary and saints as mentioned in item 11 above? Could Mary and the saints hear prayers prior to 600 AD? Is it possible for humans in heaven to hear the prayers of other humans on earth? Can that idea be supported by Scripture?

These are questions that were asked by Martin Luther in the mid-16th century. These questions caused the Protestant Reformation. The ultimate deal breaker for Martin Luther was the "sale of indulgences" for sin (item 26). His ultimate question was, "Can a man on earth, appointed by men, grant permission to violate God by sinning?" All of this was done to raise money to build Saint Peter's Basilica in Rome. Martin Luther could not justify this practice from Scripture, and therefore rejected it so vehemently that others followed his lead and revolted against the Catholic Church and the Pope. Now we have Protestants.

One surefire defense against these kinds of questions was offset by the "Church" in 1545 (item 37). "Tradition" was promoted to the lofty position of becoming equal with Scripture. *There, that solves that problem!* That invention gave the "Church" the necessary authority to do as it pleases. It sounds dangerous doesn't it? Shouldn't God have some say in religion? **He doesn't!**

From a religious standpoint, is the list of *inventions* just incidental religion, or are they dangerous practices leading people away from God? This is how religion in general evolves beyond truth.

Is God a Genius or What?

Isaiah 40:28

"Have you not known? Have you not heard? The everlasting God, the LORD, The Creator of the ends of the earth, Neither faints nor is weary. His understanding is unsearchable."

Since religion is man made, does it include God? The simplest answer is that God does not fit into religion because worship of God is a "God thing". Religion is man trying to reach God; however, it is God who reaches down to man. The early Old Testament practices were designed by God and instituted by God to demonstrate His purposes. The practices did not include any man-initiated ideas.

After being a student of the Bible for more than 50 years, I have drawn a giant conclusion. The over-arching theme of the universe is that God is love, I John 4:8 *"God is love."* A serious student of the Bible is always taught that the most important aspect of Bible interpretation is CONTEXT. One must always consider the context when reading any portion of Scripture. Who is speaking? To whom are they speaking? What is the culture of the day? What are the circumstances under which the passage is spoken or written?

Humans

70

A classic illustration of this could be found in Revelation 21:1 *"Now I saw a new heaven and a new earth, for the first heaven and the first earth had passed away. Also there was no more sea."* In the verses that follow there is a list of things that no longer exist in the new heaven: fear, crying, tears, and pain. What is meant by the "sea" no longer being in John's vision? Perhaps the interpretation can be found within the idea of "context." The Book of Revelation was written by the Apostle John. He was the only Apostle who was not martyred for his faith. Attempts were made to have him killed, but he survived each time. Finally, John was exiled to an island called Patmos. Now ask yourself what the sea might have represented to a person exiled on an island. It would have represented separation: separation from family, the things that he loved, comfort and peace. That should be considered when reading Revelation 21.

In an attempt to understand the program of God, the context of God must be established. Again, I believe that the entire universe and everything that happens does so within the context that *God is love*.

If that is the case, and since God has always existed, what was God's love like before man was created? One would have felt loved just by being around Him. But there were no people, only angelic beings. These beings were created by God for service to God in Heaven. It would not have been at all challenging for God to love these created beings. Man, however, was created with a sin nature.

> *Ephesians 2:3 ", And you He made alive, who were dead in trespasses and sins, , in which you once walked according to the course of this world, according to the prince of the power of the air, the spirit who now works in the sons of disobedience, , among whom also we all once conducted ourselves in the lusts of our flesh, fulfilling the desires of the flesh and of the mind, and were by nature children of wrath, just as the others."*

The question is always asked, "Why would God allow sin in the first place?" I believe the answer is that God is love, and He allowed man to be difficult to love. Loving man would be a huge stretch from loving other created beings.

Satan was even allowed to tempt man. It was all done with the permission of God.

> *Genesis 3: , Now the serpent was more cunning than any beast of the field which the LORD God had made. And he said to the woman, "Has God indeed said, 'You shall not eat of every tree of the garden'?" , And the woman said to the serpent, "We may eat the fruit of the trees of the garden; , but of the fruit of the tree which is in the midst of the garden, God has said, 'You shall not eat it, nor shall*

you touch it, lest you die.'" · Then the serpent said to the
woman, "You will not surely die. · For God knows that in
the day you eat of it your eyes will be opened, and you
will be like God, knowing good and evil."

Job 1: · Now there was a day when the sons of God came
to present themselves before the LORD, and Satan⁽ᵇ⁾ also
came among them. · And the LORD said to Satan, "From
where do you come?" So Satan answered the LORD and
said, "From going to and fro on the earth, and from
walking back and forth on it."
· Then the LORD said to Satan, "Have you considered My
servant Job, that there is none like him on the earth, a
blameless and upright man, one who fears God and shuns
evil?" So Satan answered the LORD and said, "Does Job
fear God for nothing? » Have You not made a hedge
around him, around his household, and around all that he
has on every side? You have blessed the work of his
hands, and his possessions have increased in the land. »
But now, stretch out Your hand and touch all that he has,
and he will surely curse You to Your face!"

In the above passage from Job, can you see how God offered Job
to Satan for temptation? God said to Satan, "Have you considered
Job?" Satan said essentially, "Give me the chance to tempt him
and he will cave in." God said, "OK." It is always like that in
human history. Satan can have no power over man unless God

grants it. God allowed evil to enter the world. There would be no measuring stick for good without evil. Evil actually has a benefit for man. There could not be any courage without fear, an evil. There could not be any joy without grief, an evil. There could not be love without hate. There is always a greater good than the evil present. It's God's plan.

From the Garden of Eden forward, man's sin nature was so powerful that man constantly failed. Choice was one of God's great gifts to man and, time after time, man would choose evil and freely justify it. It was not because he would make good choices, but because it would naturally create more of a need for God. God always had intended to demonstrate His great love by intervening into the life of man.

It wasn't bad enough that man was a sinner; God made moral and spiritual laws so stiff that man could not keep God's laws. Man would constantly fail to reach God's standards.

> *Romans 3:20 " Therefore by the deeds of the law no flesh will be justified in His sight, for by the law is the knowledge of sin."*

> *Romans 3:23 " for all have sinned and fall short of the glory of God*

Could it get any worse than man always failing and breaking God's unachievable laws? Yes! God placed the penalty of death on man's failings so that man was *hopelessly* lost. God had to actually invent death for this experience.

> *Romans 5:12 "Therefore, just as through one man sin entered the world, and death through sin, and thus death spread to all men, because all sinned"*

> *Romans 6:23 "For the wages of sin is death"*

Man's condition became so bad that existence was impossible without God. *Then* God could show the extent of His love. Jesus said that there is a level of love that transcends all other love. The highest level is that one would willingly die for another.

> *John 15:13 "**Greater love** hath no man than this, that a man lay down his life for his friends."*

God had permitted man to reach such an awful state, so that He could demonstrate His great love by dying for him. To what depths would God go to die for man?

> *Romans 5:7-8 "For scarcely for a righteous man will one die; yet perhaps for a good man someone would even dare to die. · But God demonstrates His own love toward us, in that while we were still sinners, Christ died for us."*

God made the greatest demonstration that could ever be made by dying for man in his absolutely worst state, in his most needy situation, and under the unpardonable penalty of death. For the terrible offenses of man, someone must pay the ultimate price and die.

It all was accomplished by a miraculous act.

> *John 3:16 "For God so loved the world that He gave His only begotten Son, that whoever believes in Him should not perish but have everlasting life. ₁₇ For God did not send His Son into the world to condemn the world, but that the world through Him might be saved."*

"For God," -- the greatest being in the history of the universe, "so loved" -- the greatest love ever possible, "the world" -- the greatest number ever loved, "that He gave His Son" -- the greatest gift ever known, "that whoever believes in Him" -- the SIMPLEST requirement possible, "should not perish" -- the most awful destiny know to man, "but have everlasting life" -- the greatest consolation possible.

Who was this Jesus? Did God have a son? How could that be?

> *I Timothy 3:16 "without controversy great is the mystery of godliness: God was manifested in the flesh, Justified in the Spirit, Seen by angels, Preached among the Gentiles, Believed on in the world, Received up in glory."*

It was God Himself that became flesh, injecting Himself into the world and condescending from His highly-deserved lofty position and entering the cesspool of the sin-cursed world that man had created. His reach was truly DOWN to man.

> *Philippians 2:5-8 ", Let this mind be in you which was also in Christ Jesus, , who, being in the form of God, did not consider it robbery to be equal with God, , but made Himself of no reputation, taking the form of a bondservant, and coming in the likeness of men. , And being found in appearance as a man, He humbled Himself and became obedient to the point of death, even the death of the cross. "*

How could God possibly show His love to man in any greater measure? He lowered Himself to become man, and not only man, but a servant of no reputation. He even allowed Himself to experience the death that He had created. But wait, not a nice polite death, but a horrible one, on the cross. Oh, what condescension! Oh, what love! God, in the form of Jesus, went to the cruel cross, allowing Himself to experience the pain and shame of it, all for me and you. Brilliant!

IT GETS BETTER.

He didn't stay dead. He proved His power over death and rose from the dead as He Himself had foretold.

John 20: "₁₁ But Mary stood outside by the tomb weeping, and as she wept she stooped down and looked into the tomb. ₁₂ And she saw two angels in white sitting, one at the head and the other at the feet, where the body of Jesus had lain. ₁₃ Then they said to her, "Woman, why are you weeping?"

She said to them, "Because they have taken away my Lord, and I do not know where they have laid Him." ₁₄ Now when she had said this, she turned around and saw Jesus standing there, and did not know that it was Jesus. ₁₅ Jesus said to her, "Woman, why are you weeping? Whom are you seeking?"

She, supposing Him to be the gardener, said to Him, "Sir, if You have carried Him away, tell me where You have laid Him, and I will take Him away." ₁₆ Jesus said to her, "Mary!" She turned and said to Him, "Rabboni!" (which is to say, Teacher). ₁₇ Jesus said to her, "Do not cling to Me, for I have not yet ascended to My Father; but go to My brethren and say to them, 'I am ascending to My Father and your Father, and to My God and your God.'"

God through Jesus conquered death! **This transcends religion.** Man cannot invent a tradition that can match this impossible act. **This changes everything!** Why would anyone cling to some fruitless religion (clouds without water) when he can have a relationship with this incredible, awesome, never-changing, consistent, LOVING, God? This is more than brilliant. This is Godly!

Angels couldn't believe it.

> *I Peter 1: "₁₀ Of this salvation the prophets have inquired and searched carefully, who prophesied of the grace that would come to you, ₁₁ searching what, or what manner of time, the Spirit of Christ who was in them was indicating when He testified beforehand the sufferings of Christ and the glories that would follow. ₁₂ To them it was revealed that, not to themselves, but to us₍₁₎ they were ministering the things which now have been reported to you through those who have preached the gospel to you by the Holy Spirit sent from heaven—things which angels desire to look into."*

Can you imagine the conversation in Heaven as angels said among themselves, "He never died for us. He never showed love like this to us. Yet he died for these dirty, substandard, sinful *people*." It's simply amazing!

How can a person believe this?

God thought of everything. He gave guideposts all along the way. Everything that He would do over the centuries regarding the salvation of lost man, He demonstrated over and over several thousand years PRIOR to it happening. He hinted to what He would do as early as the Garden of Eden.

Genesis 3:15 " ₁₅And I will put enmity Between you and the woman, And between your seed and her Seed; He shall bruise your head, And you shall bruise His heel. "

As God spoke directly to Satan in the garden, He alluded to a cosmic struggle that would occur between two "seeds," that of Satan (evil) and Woman (Jesus, good). This is the only place in the Bible that refers to the "seed of woman." All other *human* references would be called the "seed of man." This "seed" would not be from man, but from God through the Holy Spirit.

Matthew 1: ₁₈ "Now the birth of Jesus Christ was as follows: After His mother Mary was betrothed to Joseph, before they came together, she was found with child of the Holy Spirit. ₁₉ Then Joseph her husband, being a just man, and not wanting to make her a public example, was minded to put her away secretly. ₂₀ But while he thought about these things, behold, an angel of the Lord appeared to him in a dream, saying, "Joseph, son of David, do not be afraid to take to you Mary your wife, for that which is conceived in her is of the Holy Spirit. ₂₁ And she will bring forth a Son, and you shall call His name JESUS, for He will save His people from their sins. "

He even mentioned a less-than-permanent wound, "heel," in Genesis 3 above, that would be inflicted on Jesus (the cross).

Then God instituted the priesthood to demonstrate the ultimate actions of Jesus as mediator. He instituted a sacrifice that would show that the ultimate sacrifice (Jesus) would give Himself to die. He directed Moses to build a ceremonial tabernacle that in every way would demonstrate Jesus. Even the colors used represented some characteristic of Jesus (red represented the blood that would be shed). Jesus Himself said that the entire process was about Him.

> *Hebrews 10:7 "Then I said, 'Behold, I have come— In the volume of the book it is written of Me— To do Your will, O God.'"*

God even foretold events that would happen centuries before they took place. This is what we call prophecy. There were actually over 300 direct prophecies, including many details of the life and events of the life of Jesus, as many as 1,400 years before they happened. Look to the Internet and search for "300 Bible prophecies about Jesus."

The list below shows a few of the Old Testament (before Christ) prophecies about Jesus on the left, a brief description in the middle, followed by the New Testament (during the life of Jesus) fulfillment on the right.

Genesis 3:15.....Seed of a woman (virgin birth)..... Matthew 1:18-20
Genesis 9:26-27...The God of Shem will be the Son of Shem...Luke 3:36

Genesis 12:3...As Abraham's seed, will bless all nations...Acts 3:25,26

Psalms 22:1...Forsaken because of sins of others...2 Corinthians 5:21

Psalms 22:1...Words spoken from Calvary, "My God..." Mark 15:34

Psalms 22:2...Darkness upon Calvary...Matthew 27:45

Psalms 22:7...Total disrespect...Matthew 27:39

Psalms 22:8.."He trusted God, let Him deliver Him "...Matthew 27:43

Psalms 22:9......Born the Savior......Luke 2:7

Psalms 22:14...Died of a broken (ruptured) heart...John 19:34

Psalms 22:14,15...Suffered agony on Calvary...Mark 15:34-37

Psalms 22:15........He thirsted........John 19:28

Psalms 22:16...Hands and feet pierced....John 19:34,37;20:27

Psalms 22:17,18...Stripped Him before men...Luke 23:34,35

Psalms 22:18.....They parted His garments......John 19:23,24

Psalms 22:20,21...He committed Himself to God...Luke23:46

Psalms 22:20,21..Satan bruising the Redeemer's heel.. Hebrews 2:14

Psalms 22:22.....His Resurrection declared.....John 20:17

Psalms 22:27...He shall be the governor of the nations...Col 1:16

Psalms 22:31......"It is finished"......John 19:30

Isaiah 7:14...To be born of a virgin...Luke 1:35

Isaiah 7:14...To be Emmanuel-God with us... Matthew 1:18-23

Isaiah 8:8...Called Emmanuel...Matthew 28:20

Isaiah 9:6...A child born-Humanity...Luke 1:31

Isaiah 9:6...A Son given-Deity...Luke 1:32; John 1;14; 1 Tim. 3:16

Isaiah 9:6...Declared to be the Son of God with power... Romans. 1:3,4

Isaiah 9:6...The Wonderful One, Peleh...Luke 4:22

Isaiah 9:6...The Counselor, Yaatz...Matthew 13:54

Isaiah 9:6...The Mighty God, El Gibor...Matthew 11:20

Isaiah 9:6...The Everlasting Father, Avi Adth...John 8:58

Isaiah 9:6...The Prince of Peace, Sar Shalom...John . 16:33

Isaiah 53:1...His people would not believe Him... John 12:37-38

Isaiah 53:2a...He would grow up in a poor family.... Luke 2:7

Isaiah 53:2b...Appearance of an ordinary man... Phil. 2:7-8

Isaiah 53:3a...Despised.... Luke 4:28-29

Isaiah 53:3b...Rejected... Matthew 27:21-23

Isaiah 53:3c...Great sorrow and grief... Luke 19:41-42

Isaiah 53:3d...Men hide from association with Him... Mark 14:50-52

Isaiah 53:4a...He would have a healing ministry... Luke 6:17-19

Isaiah 53:4b...He would bear the sins of the world... 1 Pet. 2:24

Isaiah 53:4c...Thought to be cursed by God... Matthew 27:41-43

Isaiah 53:5a...Bears penalty for mankind's transgressions... Luke 23:33

Isaiah 53:5b...His sacrifice provides peace Col. 1:20

Isaiah 53:5c...His back would be whipped... Matthew 27:26

Isaiah 53:6a...He would bear the sin for all mankind...Galatians 1:4

Isaiah 53:6b...It is God's will that He bears sin debt .. 1 John 4:10

Isaiah 53:7a...Oppressed and afflicted... Matthew 27:27-31

Isaiah 53:7b...Silent before his accusers... Matthew 27:12-14

Isaiah 53:7c...Sacrificial lamb... John 1:29

Isaiah 53:8a...Confined and persecuted... Matthew 26:47-27:31

Isaiah 53:8b...He would be judged... John 18:13-22

Isaiah 53:8c...Killed.... Matthew 27:35

Isaiah 53:8d...Dies for the sins of the world... 1 John 2:2

Isaiah 53:9a...Buried in a rich man's grave... Matthew 27:57

Isaiah 53:9b...Innocent and had done no violence... Mark 15:3

Isaiah 53:9c...No deceit in his mouth... John 18:38

Isaiah 53:10a...God's will that He die for mankind... John 18:11

Isaiah 53:10b...An offering for sin... Matthew 20:28

Isaiah 53:10c...Resurrected and live forever.... Mark 16:6

Isaiah 53:10d...He would prosper... John 17:1-5

Isaiah 53:11a...God fully satisfied with His suffering... John 12:27

Isaiah 53:11b...God's servant... Romans. 5:18-19

Isaiah 53:11c...He would justify man before God... Romans. 5:8-9

Isaiah 53:11d...The sin-bearer for all mankind... Hebrews 9:28

Isaiah 53:12a...Exalted by God by of his sacrifice... Matthew 28:18

Isaiah 53:12b...He would give up his life to save mankind... Luke 23:46

Isaiah 53:12c...Grouped with criminals... Luke 23:32

Isaiah 53:12d...Sin-bearer for all mankind... 2 Corinthians 5:21

Isaiah 53:12e...Intercede to God in behalf of mankind... Luke 23:34

Dan. 9:24a...To make an end to sins... Galatians 1:3-5

Dan. 9:24b...He would be holy... Luke 1:35

Dan. 9:25...Announced to his people 483 years, to the exact day, after the decree to rebuild the city of Jerusalem... John 12:12-13

Dan. 9:26a... Messiah killed... Matthew 27:35

Dan. 9:26b...Die for the sins of the world... Hebrews 2:9

Dan. 9:26c...Killed before temple destruction... Matthew 27:50-51

Micah 4:1-8...The Kingdom established - place of Birth Bethlehem...Luke 1:33, Matthew 2:1, Luke 2:4,10,11

Micah 5:2a...Born in Bethlehem... Matthew 2:1-2

Micah 5:2b...God's servant... John 15:10

Micah 5:2c...from everlasting... John 8:58

God's main purpose in giving these prophecies was to close the door to speculation about who the "promised one" was. Not just anyone could show up and say that he was the promised one; he had to fulfill the prophecies for validation. Jesus alone fits the bill.

Jesus used this information to prove His credentials. In Luke 24, Jesus appeared after His resurrection from the dead to two travelers on a seven-mile journey (the road to Emmaus). The two men did not recognize Jesus mainly because they were not expecting to meet someone who was previously dead. During their conversation Jesus used the prophecies to prove His Messiahship.

> *Luke 24: 25-27 "₂₅ Then He said to them, "O foolish ones, and slow of heart to believe in all that the prophets have spoken! ₂₆ Ought not the Christ to have suffered these things and to enter into His glory?" ₂₇ And beginning at Moses and all the Prophets, He expounded to them in all the Scriptures the things concerning Himself."*

It was brilliant of God to provide in ADVANCE enough details of the birth, life, death and resurrection of Jesus that He was proven unmistakably to be the promised one. Unmistakably, that is, unless one has been blinded by his religion or his own prejudice.

Peter and Stephen both used this proof.

After Jesus was transported to Heaven (Acts 1), Peter spoke to a multitude of people and used the same method of proving that Jesus was the promised one. Stephen did the same thing in Acts 7. Prophecy sets the Bible apart from books of religion.

Is God a genius? No, of course God is not a genius. "Genius" is a man-made measure that some men have achieved. *God is God!* That puts Him way above genius.

Man is Hopelessly Religious

What lies behind us and what lies before us are tiny matters compared to what lies within us. – Ralph Waldo Emerson

God has placed within the heart of man a natural propensity to seek Him. That is part of being human and being made in the image of God. Have you ever seen a dog looking up into the sky trying to figure out if there is a God? Of course not! It's not part of a dog's nature to wonder about God. It *is* man's nature to have a God interest. Even atheists have a God interest. In fact, if there were no God, there wouldn't be atheists. The basis of atheism is surely God.

God also has given man a sin nature. Man will sin. Man will feed his own pride. Man will arrogantly believe that he has things figured out. With these two truths staring at each other in opposition, a natural conflict is experienced.

> *Galatians 5: "[17] For the flesh lusts (fights) against the Spirit, and the Spirit against the flesh; and these are contrary to one another, so that you do not do the things that you wish. [18] But if you are led by the Spirit, you are not under the law."*

"From the moment a man becomes aware of God as God and of himself as self, the terrible alternative of choosing God or self for the centre (of his life) is opened to him." –C.S. Lewis

With this battle pervasive within each of us, the results could go in a couple of directions. Only one of these directions is toward God and is spiritual. Another natural tendency is for man to try to understand God, or even put God into a philosophic box that is more manageable.

"God is not who you think He is; He is who He says He is". – Clarice Fluitt

This is where religion is created within the heart of man. In his quest to control his own destiny, man begins to wrap religion around the idea of God. Then the downhill slide begins.

In the Old Testament, when David was king (1000 BC), he had a very serious heart for God. He was following the pattern he was taught from the God-driven experiences of Moses (1400 BC). Remember, God had laid down the pattern through Moses for the practices that would constantly point to Jesus.

Solomon, David's son and second king of Israel, let himself be drawn away from God.

> *I Kings 11:* *"But King Solomon loved many foreign women, as well as the daughter of Pharaoh: women of the*

Moabites, Ammonites, Edomites, Sidonians, and Hittites— ² from the nations of whom the LORD had said to the children of Israel, "You shall not intermarry with them, nor they with you. Surely they will turn away your hearts after their gods." Solomon clung to these in love. ³ And he had seven hundred wives, princesses, and three hundred concubines; and his wives turned away his heart. ⁴ For it was so, when Solomon was old, that his wives turned his heart after other gods; and his heart was not loyal to the LORD his God, as was the heart of his father David. ⁵ For Solomon went after Ashtoreth the goddess of the Sidonians, and after Milcom the abomination of the Ammonites. ⁶ Solomon did evil in the sight of the LORD, and did not fully follow the LORD, as did his father David."

Over time, religion always evolves into becoming more religious. We already have discussed Solomon's son, Rehoboam, and his adversary, Jeroboam. Jeroboam invented his own religion in order to retain his leadership over the divided kingdom, II Kings 12:25-33 (chapter 2 of this book). At the spiritual level, things got bad, really bad, in the "religious" practices of Israel. Within the next 300 years, things became so spiritually corrupt that God allowed the northern kingdom to be overrun by another nation, Assyria. "Religion" generally dominated the practices of the people, and it was even initiated by the "religion's" *leaders*. God

90

finally had enough, and He allowed the southern kingdom also to be overrun, and its best people taken captive (around 600 BC).

This is important!

Even though "religion" can lead people astray, not **everyone** goes astray. The Bible is very plain that God always will have a remnant, a group of people seeking His heart.

> *Isaiah 11: "* *16* *And there shall be an highway for the remnant of his people, which shall be left, from Assyria; like as it was to Israel in the day that he came up out of the land of Egypt."*

Without further explanation, here are some of the people who God considered His remnant during the above-mentioned captivity: Daniel, Nehemiah, Ezra, and many of the other Minor Prophets.

By 400 BC, the last of the prophets, Malachi, had spoken from God to the nation of Israel. The Old Testament had been written. Within the next 400 years, until Jesus would be born, the nation had no prophet, no revelation from God, only silence. God allowed the people to go their own way spiritually, without His intervention. Those 400 years contain much well-known world history, and are called the inter-testament period, or the period of time between the Old and New Testaments. Bear in mind that the people of Israel knew the right God and had the right Book (the Bible). Their ancestry was right. Their history was right. The link back to Adam and Abraham, who both walked with God, was their link. However, the 400 years of silence from God gave the religion (now called Judaism) time to flourish. The following references to the religious development of the nation of Israel will come from Alfred Edersheim, (1993). *The Life and Times of Jesus the Messiah.* Peabody, MA: Hendrickson Publishers, Inc.

Religion developed rapidly between the Testaments.

As one would expect, the religious people began to loudly express their own opinions about the way their religion should develop. Their religion split along philosophical lines. "Denominations" developed into groups within the Jewish religious community: Pharisees, Sadducees, Essenes, and the Zealots.

Pharisees were the conservative fundamentalists of Judaism, as opposed to Sadducees, who were the liberals during this time. A Pharisee was called "rabbi."

> *Matt.23:7 "greetings in the marketplaces, and to be called by men, 'Rabbi, Rabbi.'"*

In the absence of divine revelation, the Pharisees constructed a system to reach God which centered on developing strict rules of conduct which became known as the "traditions of the elders."

> *Matt.15:2: "Why do Your disciples transgress the tradition of the elders? For they do not wash their hands when they eat bread."*

> *Matt. 7:3-5 "And why do you look at the speck in your brother's eye, but do not consider the plank in your own eye? ⁴ Or how can you say to your brother, 'Let me remove the speck from your eye'; and look, a plank is in your own eye? ⁵ Hypocrite! First remove the plank from your own eye, and then you will see clearly to remove the speck from your brother's eye."*

These traditions were originally oral, but after the fall of Jerusalem in AD 70, they would be codified in the Mishnah (affectionately known as the "Oral Torah"), the Gemara (written discussions about the Mishnah), and the Talmud (consisting of both the Mishnah and the Gemara), finished in the 4th century AD. The Pharisees esteemed these traditions **more** highly than the Word of God.

> *Matt.15:3-9 "He answered and said to them, "Why do you also transgress the commandment of God because of*

*your tradition? ⁴ For God commanded, saying, 'Honor
your father and your mother';[a] and, 'He who curses
father or mother, let him be put to death.'[b] ⁵ But you say,
'Whoever says to his father or mother, "Whatever profit
you might have received from me is a gift to God"— ⁶
then he need not honor his father or mother.'[c] Thus you
have made the commandment[d] of God of no effect by your
tradition. ⁷ Hypocrites! Well did Isaiah prophesy about
you, saying: 'These people draw near to Me with their
mouth, And[e]honor Me with their lips, But their heart is
far from Me. And in vain they worship Me, Teaching as
doctrines the commandments of men."*

*Matt. 7:8-9, 13 For everyone who asks receives, and he
who seeks finds, and to him who knocks it will be opened.
⁹ Or what man is there among you who, if his son asks for
bread, will give him a stone? .....¹³ "Enter by the narrow
gate; for wide is the gate and broad is the way that leads
to destruction, and there are many who go in by it."*

The traditions included strict regulations on Sabbath (seventh day, day of rest) conduct, such as:

A. Redefining "work" to the extent that one could hardly fetch livestock from a ditch.

*Matt.12:11 "Then He said to them, "What man is
there among you who has one sheep, and if it falls*

into a pit on the Sabbath, will not lay hold of it and lift it out?"

Luke 14:5 "Then He answered them, saying, "Which of you, having a donkey[b] or an ox that has fallen into a pit, will not immediately pull him out on the Sabbath day?"

B. A person could not walk more than 1/2 mile on the Sabbath.

C. By their definition of "work," miracles of God were not allowed on the Sabbath

Matt.12:10 "And behold, there was a man who had a withered hand. And they asked Him, saying, "Is it lawful to heal on the Sabbath?"—that they might accuse Him."

Luke 6:7 "So the scribes and Pharisees watched Him closely, whether He would heal on the Sabbath, that they might find an accusation against Him."

Luke 14:3 "And Jesus, answering, spoke to the lawyers and Pharisees, saying, "Is it lawful to heal on the Sabbath?"

John 9:16 *"Therefore some of the Pharisees said, "This Man is not from God, because He does not keep the Sabbath." Others said, "How can a man who is a sinner do such signs?" And there was a division among them."*

d. There were rules on how much work one could exert preparing meals or gathering grain.

Matt.12:2 "And when the Pharisees saw it, they said to Him, "Look, Your disciples are doing what is not lawful to do on the Sabbath!"

Luke 6:1-2 "Now it happened on the second Sabbath after the first that He went through the grain fields. And His disciples plucked the heads of grain and ate them, rubbing them in their hands. ² And some of the Pharisees said to them, "Why are you doing what is not lawful to do on the Sabbath?"

Then there were rules on washing hands before and after meals.
Matt.15:2 "Why do Your disciples transgress the tradition of the elders? For they do not wash their hands when they eat bread."

Mark 7:2-3 "Now when[a] they saw some of His disciples eat bread with defiled, that is, with unwashed hands, they found fault. , For the Pharisees and all the Jews do not eat unless they wash their hands in a special way, holding the tradition of the elders."

Luke 11:38 "When the Pharisee saw it, he marveled that He had not first washed before dinner."

There were rules about washing eating utensils and vessels.

Mark 7:4 "When they come from the marketplace, they do not eat unless they wash. And there are many other things which they have received and hold, like the washing of cups, pitchers, copper vessels, and couches."

Luke 11:39 "Then the Lord said to him, "Now you Pharisees make the outside of the cup and dish clean, but your inward part is full of greed and wickedness."

The Pharisees fasted on Tuesdays and Thursdays to commemorate Moses' traditional ascent and descent from Mt. Sinai.

Matt.9:14 "Then the disciples of John came to Him, saying, "Why do we and the Pharisees fast often, but Your disciples do not fast?"

Luke 5:33 "Then they said to Him, "Why do[c] the disciples of John fast often and make prayers, and likewise those of the Pharisees, but Yours eat and drink?"

They established a system of the secular and sacred by designating as "sinners" those who did not follow *their* traditions.

Matt.9:11 "And when the Pharisees saw it, they said to His disciples, "Why does your Teacher eat with tax collectors and sinners?"

Luke 5:30 "And their scribes and the Pharisees[a] complained against His disciples, saying, "Why do You eat and drink with tax collectors and sinners?"

Luke 7:34-39 "The Son of Man has come eating and drinking, and you say, 'Look, a glutton and a winebibber, a friend of tax collectors and sinners!' " But wisdom is justified by all her children." Then one of the Pharisees asked Him to eat with him. And He went to the Pharisee's house, and sat down to eat. " And behold, a woman in the city who was a sinner, when she knew that Jesus sat at the table in the Pharisee's house, brought an alabaster flask of fragrant oil, ⁑ and stood at His feet behind Him weeping; and she began to wash His feet with her tears, and wiped them with the hair of her head; and she kissed His feet and anointed them with the fragrant oil."

Luke15:2 "And the Pharisees and scribes complained, saying, "This Man receives sinners and eats with them."

Luke 18:9 "Also He spoke this parable to some who trusted in themselves that they were righteous, and despised others"

Synagogue (a meeting place for their religious practices) worship came to the forefront during this time. Since no one could walk more than a half mile on the Sabbath, everyone had to live within a half mile of a synagogue. If a synagogue could be built within a half mile of at least 10 families, one was built, and the Pharisees expected everyone else to move within 1/2 mile of one.

The Corban gimmick came into play where a Pharisee could pronounce as "Corban" (or dedicated to God) anything that they did not want to give or share with their parents--in effect, exempting themselves from the Fifth Commandment.

Matt.15:5 "But you say, 'Whoever says to his father or mother, "Whatever profit you might have received from me is a gift to God"

Mark 7:11 "But you say, 'If a man says to his father or mother, "Whatever profit you might have received from me is Corban"—' (that is, a gift to God)"

The Pharisees even had a system of demonic deliverance.

Matt.12:27 "And if I cast out demons by Beelzebub, by whom do your sons cast them out? Therefore they shall be your judges."

Luke 11:19 "And if I cast out demons by Beelzebub, by whom do your sons cast them out? Therefore they will be your judges."

The Pharisees "decided" that Moses was given more than the written law from God. The "oral" law was deemed equal to the written law, even though it required much interpretation.

To justify their own religion, the oral law made Jews more "special" than the gentiles (non-Jewish), who were plainly labeled sinners.

It was further "decided" that Adam was created by God already circumcised after the tradition of Moses. Therefore it was deemed a part of divine design and all others were forever considered inferior.

Legends about Jewish tradition were supposedly delivered to the patriarchs who came from Shem who "actually" had a rabbinic tribunal (a group of rabbis or religious men who debated right and wrong).

Between the testaments were 400 years of other social and religious evolution:

- The Persian Period, Darius, Artaxerxes 400-333 BC.
- Alexander the Great, 330-328 BC conquered the world, Greek became the main language.
- Greek philosophers: Aristotle, Plato, and Socrates. Homer had already written The Iliad (a poem about the Trojan wars), and The Odyssey (a story of Ulysses' 10-year journey home from Troy).
- The Ptolemies, a branch of Alexander the Great, ruled 301-198 BC.
- Antiochus IV Epiphanes, December 25, 163 BC, sacrificed a pig on the altar in the temple of Jerusalem, violating the religious sensitivities of the Jews who were forbidden from owning or eating pigs.

- Hanukkah. Three years later the temple was finally cleansed of the blood of the aforementioned pigs.
- The Maccabean Hasmonaean dynasty, 166-63 BC.
- The Romans, 63 BC Palestine came under Roman rule.
- Apocryphal books written, inter-testament books recording some Jewish history.
- The Septuagint was written (Hebrew Bible texts translated into Greek reflecting the Hellenistic influence).

Finally Jesus was born.

Galatians 4:4 "when the fullness of the time had come, God sent forth His Son, born of a woman, born under the law, ⁵ to redeem those who were under the law, that we might receive the adoption as sons."

The "fullness" of time, mentioned above, deals with the timeliness of the event of God entering into the world. The time was right because the people were at a very high level of frustration regarding the burdens of religion and politics. Furthermore, God had engineered world events in such a way that the message of God would be more likely received by the people.

Rome was in power, thus providing a sense of world peace. There were no global conflicts distracting the people of the world.

Since Rome was in power, the existing Roman roads allowed for easy access for a message of the Gospel to be delivered.

The Bible was available for the first time in the vernacular of the common people of the world (Greek).

A network of synagogues existed throughout the then-modern world providing for the message of Jesus to spread rapidly. This is part of the reason that God allowed for the Jewish people to become dispersed throughout the Roman Empire.

God even put into the heart of Caesar Augustus to require a census to be conducted which forced people to return to their town of birth. This event caused Joseph and Mary, the mother of Jesus, to return to Bethlehem, thus fulfilling the Biblical prophecy regarding the birthplace of Jesus.

> *Micah 5:2 " But you, Bethlehem Ephrathah, Though you are little among the thousands of Judah, Yet out of you shall come forth to Me The One to be Ruler in Israel, Whose goings forth are from of old, From everlasting."*

Once again a remnant.

Even though the nation of Israel was in a chaotic state of religious disarray, there existed a remnant that refused to become spiritually corrupted by all of the religious clamoring of the day. Some of those faithful few were Zachariah, Elizabeth, Simeon, Mary, Joseph, and even the wise men from the east, whose origin of spirituality is not fully known.

Matt. 1:18-21 "Now the birth of Jesus Christ was as follows: After His mother Mary was betrothed to Joseph, before they came together, she was found with child of the Holy Spirit. ¹⁹ Then Joseph her husband, being a just man, and not wanting to make her a public example, was minded to put her away secretly. ²⁰ But while he thought about these things, behold, an angel of the Lord appeared to him in a dream, saying, "Joseph, son of David, do not be afraid to take to you Mary your wife, for that which is conceived in her is of the Holy Spirit. ²¹ And she will bring forth a Son, and you shall call His name JESUS, for He will save His people from their sins."

Luke 1:5-6 "There was in the days of Herod, the king of Judea, a certain priest named Zacharias, of the division of Abijah. His wife was of the daughters of Aaron, and her name was Elizabeth. ⁶ And they were both righteous before God, walking in all the commandments and ordinances of the Lord blameless."

Luke 2:25-32 "And behold, there was a man in Jerusalem whose name was Simeon, and this man was just and devout, waiting for the Consolation of Israel, and the Holy Spirit was upon him. ²⁶ And it had been revealed to him by the Holy Spirit that he would not see death before he had seen the Lord's Christ. ²⁷ So he came by the Spirit into the temple. And when the parents brought in the Child Jesus, to do for Him according to the custom of the law, ²⁸ he took Him up in his arms and blessed God and said: " Lord, now You are letting Your servant depart in peace, According to Your word; For my eyes have seen Your salvation Which You have prepared before the face of all peoples, ³² A light to bring revelation to the Gentiles, And the glory of Your people Israel. "

Today the world is full of religion.

Religion is your enemy. Flee from it. Do not be fooled into a false sense of security. Do not claim a religion simply because of your parents. Look to God as He reaches down to you to redeem you out from under the condemning law of the spiritual world. Be the remnant.

Malachi 3:16-17 "Then those who feared the LORD spoke to one another, And the LORD listened and heard them; So a book of remembrance was written before Him For those who fear the

LORD And who meditate on His name. "They shall be Mine," says the LORD of hosts, "On the day that I make them My jewels."

Man left to himself will "naturally" form, or be drawn to, a religion, even if it's atheism. MAN IS INHERENTLY RELIGIOUS.

Jesus Hates Religion

Fundamentally, our Lord's message was Himself. He did not come merely to preach a Gospel; He himself is that Gospel. He did not come merely to give bread; He said, "I am the bread." He did not come merely to shed light; He said, "I am the light." He did not come merely to show the door; He said, "I am the door." He did not come merely to name a shepherd; He said, "I am the shepherd." He did not come merely to point the way; He said, "I am the way, the truth, and the life." -- J. Sidlow Baxter

God doesn't change.

The attitudes of God have never changed. When we say the attitudes of "God" we can also say the attitudes of Jesus. They are both God, and they share the same mind. In the Garden of Eden, when Adam and Eve sinned for the first time, they made an attempt to hide their shame by forming aprons from fig leaves to cover their nakedness.

Immediately God began to reveal His program for covering sin. It would be done through a sacrifice. The ultimate sacrifice would be Jesus as He went to the cross. For Adam and Eve, God killed an animal and took the skin from the animal and made coats of skin for Adam and Eve, thus making the first sacrifice.

Already mankind (Adam and Eve) was attempting to work out its own ideas for restoring itself to God and covering its own sin. It did not work because God did not accept the attempt of Adam and Eve to redeem themselves from the folly of their sin. God never does accept man's attempt to create his own redemptive payment. The payment for sin that God requires is death, and He would give Himself as that ultimate sacrifice. He would die for man.

The challenge for Jesus.

When Jesus began His public ministry, His biggest challenge was to change the minds of the people about their religion. As mentioned in the last chapter, religion was thriving following the 400 years of silence from God. One of the first public sermons preached by Jesus was the Sermon on the Mount. The overriding theme of the Sermon on the Mount as presented by Jesus (Matt. 5, 6, 7) was the heart of man. Jesus was trying to change the focus of their practices from outward display to the inner life-- the heart.

> *Matt. 5:21-24 "You have heard that it was said to those of old, 'You shall not murder, and whoever murders will be in danger of the judgment.'* 22 *But I say to you that whoever is angry with his brother without a cause shall be in danger of the judgment. And whoever says to his brother, 'Raca!' shall be in danger of the council. But whoever says, 'You fool!' shall be in danger of hell fire.* 23 *Therefore if you bring your gift to the altar, and there*

remember that your brother has something against you, ²⁴ leave your gift there before the altar, and go your way. First be reconciled to your brother, and then come and offer your gift."

Matt. 5:27-28 "You have heard that it was said to those of old, 'You shall not commit adultery.' ²⁸ But I say to you that whoever looks at a woman to lust for her has already committed adultery with her in his heart."

Jesus warned the masses about the religious leaders.

Matt. 16:6-12 " Then Jesus said to them, "Take heed and beware of the leaven of the Pharisees and the Sadducees." And they reasoned among themselves, saying, "It is because we have taken no bread." ⁸ But Jesus, being aware of it, said to them, "O you of little faith, why do you reason among yourselves because you have brought no bread? ⁹ Do you not yet understand, or remember the five loaves of the five thousand and how many baskets you took up? ¹⁰ Nor the seven loaves of the four thousand and how many large baskets you took up? ¹¹ How is it you do not understand that I did not speak to you concerning bread?—but to beware of the leaven of the Pharisees and Sadducees." ¹² Then they understood that He did not tell them to beware of the leaven of bread, but of the doctrine of the Pharisees and Sadducees."

The issue was the doctrine of the Pharisees and Sadducees. Doctrine. What is it? Doctrine is the beliefs of any particular religion, but doctrine is not necessarily "truth." In fact, with as much religion as exists in the world, it is safe to say that doctrine is rarely true.

In the above passage, Jesus was warning the people to be careful about the doctrine of the religious leaders. Religion will not help you find God. In fact, religion is a barrier between God and men. Even though the Jews were the chosen people through whom God revealed Himself for the entire world, they had indeed evolved beyond truth. It was the "leaven" or doctrine that had been wrapped around "truth" that made it dangerous for the people to follow.

Examine the following Scripture and see how the religious people attacked Jesus, or how He decried their religion. He was not a fan. It would be the religious leaders who would Jesus put to death.

The conflict with religion.

> *Matt. 9:11 "And when the Pharisees saw it, they said to His disciples, "Why does your Teacher eat with tax collectors and sinners?"*

Matt. 9:14 "Then the disciples of John came to Him, saying, "Why do we and the Pharisees fast often, but Your disciples do not fast?"

Matt. 12:2 "And when the Pharisees saw it, they said to Him, "Look, Your disciples are doing what is not lawful to do on the Sabbath!"

Matt. 12:10 "And behold, there was a man who had a withered hand. And they asked Him, saying, "Is it lawful to heal on the Sabbath? "that they might accuse Him."

Matt. 12:11 "Then He said to them, "What man is there among you who has one sheep, and if it falls into a pit on the Sabbath, will not lay hold of it and lift it out?"

Matt. 12:27 "And if I cast out demons by Beelzebub, by whom do your sons cast them out? Therefore they shall be your judges."

Matt. 15:2 "Why do Your disciples transgress the tradition of the elders? For they do not wash their hands when they eat bread."

Matt. 15:3 "He answered and said to them, "Why do you also transgress the commandment of God because of your tradition?"

Matt. 15:4 "For God commanded, saying, 'Honor your father and your mother'; and, 'He who curses father or mother, let him be put to death.'

Matt. 15:5 "But you say, 'Whoever says to his father or mother, "Whatever profit you might have received from me is a gift to God"

Matt. 15:6 'then he need not honor his father or mother.' Thus you have made the commandment of God of no effect by your tradition."

Matt. 15:7 "Hypocrites! Well did Isaiah prophesy about you, saying:"

Matt. 15:8 'These people draw near to Me with their mouth, And honor Me with their lips, But their heart is far from Me."

Matt. 15:9 "And in vain they worship Me, Teaching as doctrines the commandments of men.'"

Mark 7:2 "Now when they saw some of His disciples eat bread with defiled, that is, with unwashed hands, they found fault."

Mark 7:3 "For the Pharisees and all the Jews do not eat unless they wash their hands in a special way, holding the tradition of the elders."

Mark 7:4 "When they come from the marketplace, they do not eat unless they wash. And there are many other things which they have received and hold, like the washing of cups, pitchers, copper vessels, and couches."

Mark 7:5 "Then the Pharisees and scribes asked Him, "Why do Your disciples not walk according to the tradition of the elders, but eat bread with unwashed hands?"

Mark 7:8 "For laying aside the commandment of God, you hold the tradition of men the washing of pitchers and cups, and many other such things you do."

Mark 7:9 "He said to them, "All too well you reject the commandment of God, that you may keep your tradition."

Mark 7:11 "But you say, 'If a man says to his father or mother, "Whatever profit you might have received from me is Corban"' (that is, a gift to God),"

Mark 7:13 "making the word of God of no effect through your tradition which you have handed down. And many such things you do."

Luke 6:1 "Now it happened on the second Sabbath after the first that He went through the grain fields. And His disciples plucked the heads of grain and ate them, rubbing them in their hands."

Luke 6:2 "And some of the Pharisees said to them, "Why are you doing what is not lawful to do on the Sabbath?"

Luke 6:7 "So the scribes and Pharisees watched Him closely, whether He would heal on the Sabbath, that they might find an accusation against Him."

Luke 7:34 "The Son of Man has come eating and drinking, and you say, 'Look, a glutton and a winebibber, a friend of tax collectors and sinners!'

Luke 7:35 "But wisdom is justified by all her children."

Luke 7:36 "Then one of the Pharisees asked Him to eat with him. And He went to the Pharisee's house, and sat down to eat."

Luke 7:37 "And behold, a woman in the city who was a sinner, when she knew that Jesus sat at the table in the Pharisee's house, brought an alabaster flask of fragrant oil"

Luke 7:38 "and stood at His feet behind Him weeping; and she began to wash His feet with her tears, and wiped them with the hair of her head; and she kissed His feet and anointed them with the fragrant oil."

Luke 7:39 "Now when the Pharisee who had invited Him saw this, he spoke to himself, saying, "This Man, if He were a prophet, would know who and what manner of woman this is who is touching Him, for she is a sinner."

Luke 11:39 "Then the Lord said to him, "Now you Pharisees make the outside of the cup and dish clean, but your inward part is full of greed and wickedness."

Luke 14:3 "And Jesus, answering, spoke to the lawyers and Pharisees, saying, "Is it lawful to heal on the Sabbath?"

Luke 14:5 "Then He answered them, saying, "Which of you, having a donkey or an ox that has fallen into a pit, will not immediately pull him out on the Sabbath day?"

Luke 15:2 "And the Pharisees and scribes complained, saying, "This Man receives sinners and eats with them."

Luke 18:9 "Also He spoke this parable to some who trusted in themselves that they were righteous, and despised others:"

John 9:16 "Therefore some of the Pharisees said, "This Man is not from God, because He does not keep the Sabbath." Others said, "How can a man who is a sinner do such signs?" And there was a division among them."

The following tirade by Jesus, made directly in the presence of religious leaders, provoked them to seek out ways of doing away with Him. This statement is full to the brim with truth and judgment against the people who were leading others astray. In fact, notice verses 13 and 14 below. Jesus brings a railing accusation against the people who were supposed to help others find a relationship with God and gain Heaven. Instead, they were leading people to Hell through the teachings of their religion. Can you imagine spending your entire life sincerely steeped in your religion, and miss a relationship with God and Heaven? That *would* be a "cloud without water."

> *Matt. 23: " Then Jesus spoke to the multitudes and to His disciples, ₂ saying: "The scribes and the Pharisees sit in Moses' seat. ₃ Therefore whatever they tell you to observe that observe and do, but do not do according to their works; for they say, and do not do. ₄ For they bind heavy burdens, hard to bear, and lay them on men's shoulders; but they themselves will not move them with one of their fingers. ₅ But all their works they do to be seen by men. They make their phylacteries broad and enlarge the borders of their garments. ₆ They love the best places at feasts, the best seats in the synagogues, ₇ greetings in the marketplaces, and to be called by men, 'Rabbi, Rabbi.' ₈ But you, do not be called 'Rabbi'; for One is your Teacher, the Christ, and you are all brethren. ₉ Do not call anyone on earth your father; for One is your Father, He who is in heaven. ₁₀ And do not be called teachers; for One is your Teacher, the Christ. ₁₁ But he who is greatest among you shall be your servant. ₁₂ And whoever exalts himself will be humbled, and he who humbles himself will be exalted.*
>
> *₁₃ "But woe to you, scribes and Pharisees, hypocrites! For you shut up the kingdom of heaven against men; for you neither go in yourselves, nor do you allow those who are entering to go in. ₁₄ Woe to you, scribes and Pharisees,*

hypocrites! For you devour widows' houses, and for a pretense make long prayers. Therefore you will receive greater condemnation.¹⁵ "Woe to you, scribes and Pharisees, hypocrites! For you travel land and sea to win one proselyte, and when he is won, you make him twice as much a son of hell as yourselves. "Woe to you, blind guides, who say, 'Whoever swears by the temple, it is nothing; but whoever swears by the gold of the temple, he is obliged to perform it.' ¹⁷ Fools and blind! For which is greater, the gold or the temple that sanctifies the gold? ¹⁸ And, 'Whoever swears by the altar, it is nothing; but whoever swears by the gift that is on it, he is obliged to perform it.' ¹⁹ Fools and blind! For which is greater, the gift or the altar that sanctifies the gift? ²⁰ Therefore he who swears by the altar, swears by it and by all things on it. ²¹ He who swears by the temple, swears by it and by Him who dwells in it. ²² And he who swears by heaven, swears by the throne of God and by Him who sits on it. ²³ "Woe to you, scribes and Pharisees, hypocrites! For you pay tithe of mint and anise and cummin, and have neglected the weightier matters of the law: justice and mercy and faith. These you ought to have done, without leaving the others undone. ²⁴ Blind guides, who strain out a gnat and swallow a camel! ²⁵ "Woe to you, scribes and Pharisees, hypocrites! For you cleanse the outside of the cup and dish, but inside they are full of extortion and self-

indulgence. ²⁶ Blind Pharisee, first cleanse the inside of the cup and dish, that the outside of them may be clean also. "Woe to you, scribes and Pharisees, hypocrites! For you are like whitewashed tombs which indeed appear beautiful outwardly, but inside are full of dead men's bones and all uncleanness. ²⁸ Even so you also outwardly appear righteous to men, but inside you are full of hypocrisy and lawlessness. "Woe to you, scribes and Pharisees, hypocrites! Because you build the tombs of the prophets and adorn the monuments of the righteous, ³⁰ and say, 'If we had lived in the days of our fathers, we would not have been partakers with them in the blood of the prophets. "Therefore you are witnesses against yourselves that you are sons of those who murdered the prophets. ³² Fill up, then, the measure of your fathers' guilt. ³³ Serpents, brood of vipers! How can you escape the condemnation of hell? ³⁴ Therefore, indeed, I send you prophets, wise men, and scribes: some of them you will kill and crucify, and some of them you will scourge in your synagogues and persecute from city to city, ³⁵ that on you may come all the righteous blood shed on the earth, from the blood of righteous Abel to the blood of Zechariah, son of Berechiah, whom you murdered between the temple and the altar. ³⁶ Assuredly, I say to you, all these things will come upon this generation."

Jesus' personal encounter with the lawyer.

At the personal level, Jesus was a most skilled communicator. Why not? He is God. One day a lawyer came to see Jesus with less than pure motives. He wanted to show off his religion and mastery of the religious law. His heart was full of pride, arrogance and self-justification. He was so very typical of people of all ages throughout history, including our present day. The encounter is from a very famous passage found in Luke 10. The name of the story is known by a vast amount of people, both religious and non-religious, as "The Good Samaritan." Let's step our way through the story in Luke 10.

A direct question was asked to Jesus by a lawyer but, based on the answer given by Jesus, it is obvious that there was more in the man's heart than the simple question.

> [25] *And behold, a certain lawyer stood up and tested Him, saying, "Teacher, what shall I do to inherit eternal life?"*

Jesus answered the lawyer.

> [26] *He said to him, "What is written in the law? What is your reading of it?"*

The lawyer answered by quoting the Old Testament.

²⁷ So he answered and said, " 'You shall love the LORD your God with all your heart, with all your soul, with all your strength, and with all your mind,' and 'your neighbor as yourself.'"

Jesus outwardly dismissed the lawyer, but inwardly he knew that the encounter was anything but over.

²⁸ And He said to him, "You have answered rightly; do this and you will live."

Now it gets really interesting.

²⁹ But he, wanting to justify himself, said to Jesus, "And who is my neighbor?"

The Scripture is very direct here. The heart of the man was revealed to us so that we can understand the encounter, and comprehend the depths of the answer. It is obvious that Jesus is answering the man's heart and not just the verbal question.

³⁰ Then Jesus answered and said: "A certain man went down from Jerusalem to Jericho, and fell among thieves, who stripped him of his clothing, wounded him, and departed, leaving him half dead.

Jesus was about to skillfully attack the lawyer's religion and prejudices. The first issue is the man's religious law. In the Jewish custom, the people are allowed to help others when in need, but not everyone. The religion had divided people into classes with our lawyer friend being in the "correct" class. The main way of determining the class to which a person belonged was by his garments. The man in the parable *had* no garments. Our lawyer would be greatly conflicted by this issue. Could the lawyer help the traveler based on his understanding of the law?

Being half dead is an interesting idea here. Based on the question initially asked by the lawyer and the answers given by Jesus, I think that the issue being dealt with here is "inheriting eternal life." The man, who was half dead, spiritually speaking, was physically alive but spiritually dead.

> *31 Now by chance a certain priest came down that road. And when he saw him, he passed by on the other side. 32 Likewise a Levite, when he arrived at the place, came and looked, and passed by on the other side.*

Notice the characters in this story. I find it interesting that Jesus would tell such a long story, including these very unique people in it: a naked stranger, a priest, and, so far, a Levite. The naked man represented an attack on the lawyer's cultural prejudice. The priest represented an attack on the lawyer's religious prejudice, and the Levite was the custodian of the law. For a man spiritually dead, culture, religion and the law were impotent to help. He needed more, an act of God.

> *[33] But a certain Samaritan, as he journeyed, came where he was. And when he saw him, he had compassion.*

Now we have an ethnic issue. Jews have no dealings with Samaritans (John 4:9 *"Then the woman of Samaria said to Him (Jesus), "How is it that You, being a Jew, ask a drink from me, a Samaritan woman?" For Jews have no dealings with Samaritans."*). Without explaining the history, suffice it to say that our lawyer friend had some serious ethnic differences with Samaritans. This would surely stretch him culturally. Of all things, this Samaritan represented Jesus Himself.

> *[34] So he went to him and bandaged his wounds, pouring on oil and wine; and he set him on his own animal, brought him to an inn, and took care of him.*

This narrative represents a salvation experience. "Oil" represents the Holy Spirit, and "wine" represents joy. A *supernatural* experience must be had to connect one with God. It is not an act of religion, keeping the law, or being born into a certain culture.

Taking care of the newly-regenerated naked man is the hardest part. Making disciples is more work than making converts.

124

[35] *On the next day, when he departed,[a] he took out two denarii, gave them to the innkeeper, and said to him, 'Take care of him; and whatever more you spend, when I come again, I will repay you.'*

Not to get into eschatology (study of the end times), but please understand that the Good Samaritan (Jesus) will return one day and will reward His followers accordingly.

Now here's the painful answer to the original question asked by the lawyer:

[36] *So which of these three do you think was neighbor to him who fell among the thieves?"*

I can almost see the lawyer struggle with the ideas that had just been presented. He had all of his prejudices skillfully dissected by Jesus. He had the answer to his heart's question, "Am I alright?" The answer was, "No." He couldn't even bring himself to say, "Samaritan."

[37] *And he said, "He who showed mercy on him."* *Then Jesus said to him, "Go and do likewise."*

God had given the responsibility to these descendents of Abraham to deliver the above message to the people of the world, but they had, instead, evolved into narrow and arrogantly-religious people. Clouds they were without water.

The false hope given by religion is in direct opposition to the heart of Jesus, which desires a spiritual relationship with man. Jesus hates religion.

Paul Survived Religion

As the centuries pass, the evidence is accumulating that, measured by His effect on history, Jesus is the most influential life ever lived on this planet. -- Historian Kenneth Scott Latourette

We know that the Apostle Paul was the major writer of the New Testament. We also know that Paul initially rejected Jesus as the Messiah which, of course, later changed. What was that transition like? What did Paul say before his epiphany, and then after?

Paul was very religious.

> *Galatians 1:13 "For you have heard of my former conduct in Judaism, how I persecuted the church of God beyond measure and tried to destroy it. ¹⁴ And I advanced in Judaism beyond many of my contemporaries in my own nation, being more exceedingly zealous for the traditions of my fathers."*

> *Philippians 3:5 "circumcised the eighth day, of the stock of Israel, of the tribe of Benjamin, a Hebrew of the Hebrews; concerning the law, a Pharisee; ⁶ concerning zeal, persecuting the church; concerning the righteousness which is in the law, blameless."*

Paul was steeped in Judaism, and well indoctrinated in the traditions of the "fathers" of his religion. His heritage was enviable to Jews, and he was a proud member of one of the denominations formed during the inter-testament period, a Pharisee. He actually gloried in the fact that he was blameless of the law. He was very, very religious. We have already seen that the religion and tradition had evolved to the point that they actually opposed the Messiah. It was the case that both religion and tradition did great harm to the people, and to the purpose of Jesus. Instead of welcoming the Messiah with open arms, they challenged, resisted, and ultimately killed Him.

After the resurrection and ascension of Jesus, Paul went so far as to actually imprison and kill those who HAD believed that Jesus was the Messiah. The presence of Paul in *any* group was an extreme threat to the cause of Christ. Killing people who don't believe the way that you believe is not a new thing. In the 21st century, extreme Muslims would like to see every Christian and Jew dead. We have labeled this terrorism. Was Paul a terrorist?

Paul knew how to work his religion.

> *Acts 23:6 "But when Paul perceived that one part were Sadducees and the other Pharisees, he cried out in the council, "Men and brethren, I am a Pharisee, the son of a Pharisee; concerning the hope and resurrection of the*

dead I am being judged!" [7] *And when he had said this, a dissension arose between the Pharisees and the Sadducees; and the assembly was divided.* [8] *For Sadducees say that there is no resurrection—and no angel or spirit; but the Pharisees confess both.* [9] *Then there arose a loud outcry. And the scribes of the Pharisees' party arose and protested, saying, "We find no evil in this man; but if a spirit or an angel has spoken to him, let us not fight against God."*

After his "conversion" Paul would become a thorn in the side of the Jews. In the narrative above, Paul was accused of heresy because of "jumping ship" spiritually. He recognized that there were people of differing Jewish "denominations" in the proceedings of that public hearing. In order to divert the attention of the group away from him, he interjected his own "religious" bent. He knew that it would create religious chaos because of the doctrinal differences. It worked like a charm. It seems to be a pattern; religion creates hard feelings among its constituents.

Paul's conversion.

Acts 9:1 "Then Saul, still breathing threats and murder against the disciples of the Lord, went to the high priest [2] *and asked letters from him to the synagogues of Damascus, so that if he found any who were of the Way, whether men or women, he might bring them bound to*

130

Jerusalem. As he journeyed he came near Damascus, and suddenly a light shone around him from heaven. ⁴ Then he fell to the ground, and heard a voice saying to him, "Saul, Saul, why are you persecuting Me?" ⁵ And he said, "Who are You, Lord?" Then the Lord said, "I am Jesus, whom you are persecuting. It is hard for you to kick against the goads." ⁶ So he, trembling and astonished, said, "Lord, what do You want me to do?"

As in every conversion, Paul changed his mind and heart about the way he viewed Jesus. At one moment, he did not think that Jesus was the Messiah, and the next he did. This conversion experience is certainly not typical in that Paul had a distinctly unique encounter with Jesus. Jesus made a personal appearance to Paul, something that rarely happens in most salvation experiences. Even though each person's experience is in someway unique, each one is the same in that we have an encounter with Jesus. I have never personally heard of a person who had quite that kind of experience.

Being a student of the Bible, Paul should have known enough prophetic Scripture to connect the dots. He should have known that Jesus was the promised one, the Messiah. Perhaps Paul was giving into the peer pressure brought to bear by his fellow Jews. Perhaps religious pride kept him from acknowledging Jesus as Messiah. He may have been blinded by his own zeal. Maybe the sheer change in ceremonial practice was too much for him. Who knows why a person resists so vehemently? Without any surprise, Paul's zeal would carry over after his transformation.

What a change!

Later, when it became known that Paul had become a follower of Jesus, Paul was brought before the Jewish authorities to answer for having turned away from "Judaism." He hadn't really turned away; he wasn't a converted Jew, he was a completed Jew. The Jews should have been looking for the Messiah to come, and when He came it would only have completed the prophecy of the fathers. But these Jews did not want Messiah to come. It would require too great of a change in thinking and practice, a major paradigm shift. The following text is the answer that Paul gave for his defense of having accepted Jesus as the Messiah. It was his personal testimony.

> *Acts 22:1 "Brethren and fathers, hear my defense before you now." ² And when they heard that he spoke to them in the Hebrew language, they kept all the more silent. Then he said: ³ "I am indeed a Jew, born in Tarsus of Cilicia, but brought up in this city at the feet of Gamaliel, taught according to the strictness of our fathers' law, and was zealous toward God as you all are today. ⁴ I persecuted this Way to the death, binding and delivering into prisons both men and women, ⁵ as also the high priest*

bears me witness, and all the council of the elders, from whom I also received letters to the brethren, and went to Damascus to bring in chains even those who were there to Jerusalem to be punished. "Now it happened, as I journeyed and came near Damascus at about noon, suddenly a great light from heaven shone around me. [7] *And I fell to the ground and heard a voice saying to me, 'Saul, Saul, why are you persecuting Me?'* [8] *So I answered, 'Who are You, Lord?' And He said to me, 'I am Jesus of Nazareth, whom you are persecuting.'* [9] *"And those who were with me indeed saw the light and were afraid,*[a] *but they did not hear the voice of Him who spoke to me.* [10] *So I said, 'What shall I do, Lord?' And the Lord said to me, 'Arise and go into Damascus, and there you will be told all things which are appointed for you to do.'* [11] *And since I could not see for the glory of that light, being led by the hand of those who were with me, I came into Damascus.* [12] *"Then a certain Ananias, a devout man according to the law, having a good testimony with all the Jews who dwelt there,* [13] *came to me; and he stood and said to me, 'Brother Saul, receive your sight.' And at that same hour I looked up at him.* [14] *Then he said, 'The God of our fathers has chosen you that you should know His will, and see the Just One, and hear the voice of His mouth.* [15] *For you will be His witness to all men of what you have seen and heard.* [16] *And now why are you waiting? Arise*

and be baptized, and wash away your sins, calling on the
name of the Lord.'

Paul was uniquely qualified.

Paul had certain characteristics that made him uniquely qualified
to carry the message of Jesus to the known world. Paul was
extremely well educated in the religion of the Jews, he was very
zealous about his beliefs, and he possessed the citizenships of
both Israel and Rome. Because of his Roman citizenship, he was
naturally granted access to any country within the Roman
Empire. Perhaps these were qualities that God thought could be
useful in carrying the message throughout the empire.

> *Acts 13:1 " Now in the church that was at Antioch there*
> *were certain prophets and teachers: Barnabas, Simeon*
> *who was called Niger, Lucius of Cyrene, Manaen who*
> *had been brought up with Herod the tetrarch, and Saul.* ²
> *As they ministered to the Lord and fasted, the Holy Spirit*
> *said, "Now separate to Me Barnabas and Saul for the*
> *work to which I have called them."* ³ *Then, having fasted*
> *and prayed, and laid hands on them, they sent them away.*
> ⁴ *So, being sent out by the Holy Spirit, they went down to*
> *Seleucia, and from there they sailed to Cyprus.* ⁵ *And*
> *when they arrived in Salamis, they preached the word of*
> *God in the synagogues of the Jews. They also had John as*
> *their assistant."*

God chose Paul and Barnabas to begin a global missionary endeavor. Since Paul was a Roman citizen, he was allowed to travel at will. Being a well-educated Jew, he was also equipped to deliver a succinct message to Jews, convincing them that Jesus was the long-expected Messiah. This meager beginning would result in the 2.1 billion people in the world who would claim today to be a believer in Jesus as the Son of God.

What a quantum leap in theology for Paul. He went from a zealous, well-schooled, Jesus- hating, believer-persecuting, defender of his religion, to a rabid follower of Jesus, the Messiah. Read his message as he journeyed throughout the Middle Eastern world:

> *Acts 13:14 "But when they departed from Perga, they came to Antioch in Pisidia, and went into the synagogue on the Sabbath day and sat down. 15 And after the reading of the Law and the Prophets, the rulers of the synagogue sent to them, saying, "Men and brethren, if you have any word of exhortation for the people, say on." 16 Then Paul stood up, and motioning with his hand said, "Men of Israel, and you who fear God, listen: 17 The God of this people Israel chose our fathers, and exalted the people when they dwelt as strangers in the land of Egypt, and with an uplifted arm He brought them out of it. 18 Now for a time of about forty years He put up with their ways*

in the wilderness. ¹⁹ And when He had destroyed seven nations in the land of Canaan, He distributed their land to them by allotment. ²⁰ "After that He gave them judges for about four hundred and fifty years, until Samuel the prophet. ²¹ And afterward they asked for a king; so God gave them Saul the son of Kish, a man of the tribe of Benjamin, for forty years. ²² And when He had removed him, He raised up for them David as king, to whom also He gave testimony and said, 'I have found David the son of Jesse, a man after My own heart, who will do all My will.' ²³ From this man's seed, according to the promise, God raised up for Israel a Savior—Jesus—

Acts 15:1 "And certain men came down from Judea and taught the brethren, "Unless you are circumcised according to the custom of Moses, you cannot be saved." ² Therefore, when Paul and Barnabas had no small dissension and dispute with them, they determined that Paul and Barnabas and certain others of them should go up to Jerusalem, to the apostles and elders, about this question."

Acts 15:1-2 above demonstrates a radical change in mind for Paul. He would have been a fanatical advocate of circumcision, which was strict adherence to the laws of Moses. Prior to Jesus, Moses would have been the benchmark for religious practice.

Here Paul is perfectly willing to negate the teachings of Moses, and promote the example of Jesus. This shift in theology would make Paul an enemy of Judaism, and would result in his martyrdom.

One major stumbling block for the Jews would have been their religious expectations. They expected that the Messiah would be one who would "deliver" them from the bondage of Rome, not the bondage of sin. How could Jesus be the Messiah? After all, He was killed. That was not in keeping with their desires. Defending the idea that Messiah must have *suffered*, based on Old Testament prophecy, was the method that Jesus employed on the road to Emmaus in Luke 24. This message also fed Paul's ministry.

> *Acts 17:1 "Now when they had passed through Amphipolis and Apollonia, they came to Thessalonica, where there was a synagogue of the Jews. ² Then Paul, as his custom was, went in to them, and for three Sabbaths reasoned with them from the Scriptures, ³ explaining and demonstrating that the Christ had to suffer and rise again from the dead, and saying, "This Jesus whom I preach to you is the Christ."*

As Paul grew more and more spiritual in his zeal for God, he developed a passion to better understand Jesus. The entire concept of Jesus, God in the flesh, is rather mind boggling.

Below is a powerful expression from Paul in this burning desire to better "know."

> *Philippians 3:10 "₁₀ that I may know Him and the power of His resurrection, and the fellowship of His sufferings, being conformed to His death, ₁₁ if, by any means, I may attain to the resurrection from the dead. ₁₂ Not that I have already attained, or am already perfected; but I press on, that I may lay hold of that for which Christ Jesus has also laid hold of me. ₁₃ Brethren, I do not count myself to have apprehended; but one thing I do, forgetting those things which are behind and reaching forward to those things which are ahead, ₁₄ I press toward the goal for the prize of the upward call of God in Christ Jesus. "*

The resurrection of Jesus was a message worthy of selfless defense.

Chuck Colson in his book, Born Again, mentions a defining thought that convinced him that the resurrection of Jesus really happened. His epiphany came as a result of Watergate. He said that if only four or five people had stuck with their lies about the Watergate break-in, they would have all avoided prison. But, to the man, they all caved in under the threat of punishment. Every Apostle of Jesus went to a martyr's grave claiming that Jesus was raised from the dead. Human nature dictates that when one is under the threat of punishment or physical harm, he will abandon his story if it is not true. Paul's firm convictions that Jesus was the Messiah, the Son of God, God in the flesh, carried him throughout his ministry, even in the face of persecution.

> *Acts 13:44 "But when the Jews saw the multitudes, they were filled with envy; and contradicting and blaspheming, they opposed the things spoken by Paul."*

> *Acts 14:19 "Then Jews from Antioch and Iconium came there; and having persuaded the multitudes, they stoned Paul and dragged him out of the city, supposing him to be dead."*

> *Acts 16:22 "Then the multitude rose up together against them; and the magistrates tore off their clothes and commanded them to be beaten with rods. 23 And when they had laid many stripes on them, they threw them into prison, commanding the jailer to keep them securely. 24 Having received such a charge, he put them into the inner prison and fastened their feet in the stocks."*

> *Acts 20:24 "But none of these things move me; nor do I count my life dear to myself,[b] so that I may finish my race with joy, and the ministry which I received from the Lord Jesus, to testify to the gospel of the grace of God."*

Acts 21:32 "He immediately took soldiers and centurions, and ran down to them. And when they saw the commander and the soldiers, they stopped beating Paul."

Acts 23:1 "Then Paul, looking earnestly at the council, said, "Men and brethren, I have lived in all good conscience before God until this day." ² And the high priest Ananias commanded those who stood by him to strike him on the mouth."

II Cor. 11:24 "From the Jews five times I received forty stripes minus one. ²⁵ Three times I was beaten with rods; once I was stoned; three times I was shipwrecked; a night and a day I have been in the deep; ²⁶ in journeys often, in perils of waters, in perils of robbers, in perils of my own countrymen, in perils of the Gentiles, in perils in the city, in perils in the wilderness, in perils in the sea, in perils among false brethren; ²⁷ in weariness and toil, in sleeplessness often, in hunger and thirst, in fastings often, in cold and nakedness"

Paul minced no words about his faith.

Paul was opposed to, and wrote against, those who would accept Jesus as the Messiah, then try to revert back to the old ways of the Jews. It was a remarkable transformation.

Galatians 1:6 "I marvel that you are turning away so soon from Him who called you in the grace of Christ, to a different gospel, ⁷ which is not another; but there are some who trouble you and want to pervert the gospel of Christ. ⁸ But even if we, or an angel from heaven, preach any other gospel to you than what we have preached to you, let him be accursed. ⁹ As we have said before, so now I say again, if anyone preaches any other gospel to you than what you have received, let him be accursed."

It was our highly-educated and qualified Paul that would connect the dots for the Jews. Of course, Jews should have known that Jesus was the Messiah. For that matter, so should have Paul. Any serious student of the Old Testament, and not *religion*, should have known when, where, how, through whom, and many more details identifying Jesus as the Messiah. Paul would make the connections in a brilliant way.

Jesus was a part of the wilderness wanderings – 1400 BC.

I Cor. 10:1 "Moreover, brethren, I do not want you to be unaware that all our fathers were under the cloud, all passed through the sea, ² all were baptized into Moses in the cloud and in the sea, ³ all ate the same spiritual food, ⁴ and all drank the same spiritual drink. For they drank of that spiritual Rock that followed them, and that Rock was Christ."

Jesus is God.

*I Tim. 3:16 "And without controversy great is the mystery
of godliness: God was manifested in the flesh, Justified in
the Spirit, Seen by angels, Preached among the Gentiles,
Believed on in the world, Received up in glory."*

*Heb. 1:1-3 "God, who at various times and in various
ways spoke in time past to the fathers by the prophets, ²
has in these last days spoken to us by His Son, whom He
has appointed heir of all things, through whom also He
made the worlds; ³ who being the brightness of His glory
and the express image of His person, and upholding all
things by the word of His power, when He had by Himself
purged our sins, sat down at the right hand of the Majesty
on high"*

Jesus is greater than Moses.

*Heb. 3:1 "Therefore, holy brethren, partakers of the
heavenly calling, consider the Apostle and High Priest of
our confession, Christ Jesus, ² who was faithful to Him
who appointed Him, as Moses also was faithful in all His
house. ³ For this One has been counted worthy of more
glory than Moses, inasmuch as He who built the house
has more honor than the house."*

Jesus is the High Priest.

Heb. 4:14 "Seeing then that we have a great High Priest who has passed through the heavens, Jesus the Son of God, let us hold fast our confession. ¹⁵ For we do not have a High Priest who cannot sympathize with our weaknesses, but was in all points tempted as we are, yet without sin. ¹⁶ Let us therefore come boldly to the throne of grace, that we may obtain mercy and find grace to help in time of need."

Don't reject Jesus as the Messiah.

Heb. 6:4 "For it is impossible for those who were once enlightened, and have tasted the heavenly gift, and have become partakers of the Holy Spirit, ⁵ and have tasted the good word of God and the powers of the age to come, ⁶ if they fall away, to renew them again to repentance, since they crucify again for themselves the Son of God, and put Him to an open shame."

Jesus is Melchizedek.

Heb. 7: 1 "For this Melchizedek, king of Salem, priest of the Most High God, who met Abraham returning from the slaughter of the kings and blessed him, ² to whom also Abraham gave a tenth part of all, first being translated "king of righteousness," and then also king of Salem, meaning "king of peace," ³ without father, without mother, without genealogy, having neither beginning of days nor end of life, but made like the Son of God, remains a priest continually."

Jesus was the sacrifice.

Heb. 9:12 "Not with the blood of goats and calves, but with His own blood He entered the Most Holy Place once for all, having obtained eternal redemption. ¹³ For if the blood of bulls and goats and the ashes of a heifer, sprinkling the unclean, sanctifies for the purifying of the flesh, ¹⁴ how much more shall the blood of Christ, who through the eternal Spirit offered Himself without spot to God, cleanse your conscience from dead works to serve the living God?"

It was always about Jesus.

Heb. 10:1 "For the law, having a shadow of the good things to come, and not the very image of the things, can never with these same sacrifices, which they offer continually year by year, make those who approach perfect. ² For then would they not have ceased to be offered? For the worshipers, once purified, would have had no more consciousness of sins. ³ But in those

144

sacrifices there is a reminder of sins every year. ⁴ For it is not possible that the blood of bulls and goats could take away sins. ⁵ Therefore, when He came into the world, He said: " Sacrifice and offering You did not desire, But a body You have prepared for Me. ⁶ In burnt offerings and sacrifices for sin You had no pleasure. Then I said, behold, I have come— In the volume of the book it is written of Me— To do Your will, O God.'" ⁸ Previously saying, "Sacrifice and offering, burnt offerings, and offerings for sin You did not desire, nor had pleasure in them " (which are offered according to the law), ⁹ then He said, "Behold, I have come to do Your will, O God."₍₉₎ He takes away the first that He may establish the second. ¹⁰ By that will we have been sanctified through the offering of the body of Jesus Christ once for all."

Rejecting Jesus is very dangerous.

Heb. 10: "Anyone who has rejected Moses' law dies without mercy on the testimony of two or three witnesses. ²⁹ Of how much worse punishment, do you suppose, will he be thought worthy who has trampled the Son of God underfoot, counted the blood of the covenant by which he was sanctified a common thing, and insulted the Spirit of grace? ³⁰ For we know Him who said, "Vengeance is Mine, I will repay," says the Lord. And again, "The

LORD will judge His people." ³¹ It is a fearful thing to fall into the hands of the living God."

It all requires faith in Jesus to please God.

Heb. 11:6 "But without faith it is impossible to please Him, for he who comes to God must believe that He is, and that He is a rewarder of those who diligently seek Him."

Paul survived his religion.

Decades after Paul's conversion, he remained faithful to his conviction that Jesus was the Messiah. The passion with which he served his "religion" had been transferred to his newly-developed belief in Jesus. He was a serious follower of Jesus. During Paul's ministry and following his dramatic conversion, Paul traveled for decades throughout the Roman Empire spreading the Gospel, he wrote half of the New Testament, suffered immeasurable persecution, and ended up in a Roman prison. His life and message cannot be measured. Today his influence lives on and continues to spread as his writings are instrumental in forming the doctrine of the body of believers that today we call "the Church." (not to be confused with the Catholic Church) The satisfaction with which he met his fate can be sensed in his last writings.

II Timothy 4:6 "For I am already being poured out as a drink offering, and the time of my departure is at hand. ⁷ I have fought the good fight, I have finished the race, I have kept the faith."

Paul truly survived his religion in becoming one of the shining stars for people of faith.

Daniel 12:3 "Those who are wise shall shine Like the brightness of the firmament, And those who turn many to righteousness Like the stars forever and ever."

Satan Loves Religion

Wherever God erects a house of prayer, The Devil builds a chapel there; And 'twill be found, upon examination, The latter has the largest congregation. – Daniel Defoe

Does Satan have an interest in religion? Does Satan have any input into the development of man's religion? It can be seen from the passage below that Satan has a very unholy ambition to be as powerful as God.

> *Isaiah 14:12 "How you are fallen from heaven, O Lucifer, son of the morning! How you are cut down to the ground, You who weakened the nations!* 13 *For you have said in your heart:*
>   *' I will ascend into heaven,*
>   *I will exalt my throne above the stars of God;*
>   *I will also sit on the mount of the congregation*
>   *On the farthest sides of the north;*
>   14 *I will ascend above the heights of the clouds,*
>   *I will be like the Most High.'*

It should also be noted that a part of Satan's ambition is to have an expanded influence. Since Satan cannot harm God, the only affect that he can have is to do harm to God's creation: mankind. Since man has a propensity for spiritual expression and Satan has an ambition to rule at the spiritual level, a natural union results: "religion."

From Job chapter one we see that Satan's evil tendency is to try to separate man from God.

> *Job 1:6 "Now there was a day when the sons of God came to present themselves before the LORD, and Satan also came among them. ⁷ And the LORD said to Satan, "From where do you come?" So Satan answered the LORD and said, "From going to and fro on the earth, and from walking back and forth on it." ⁸ Then the LORD said to Satan, "Have you considered My servant Job, that there is none like him on the earth, a blameless and upright man, one who fears God and shuns evil?" ⁹ So Satan answered the LORD and said, "Does Job fear God for nothing? ¹⁰ Have You not made a hedge around him, around his household, and around all that he has on every side? You have blessed the work of his hands, and his possessions have increased in the land. ¹¹ But now, stretch out Your hand and touch all that he has, and he will surely curse You to Your face!"*

Both good and evil are at Satan's disposal.

> *Genesis 2:17 "Then the LORD God took the man and put him in the garden of Eden to tend and keep it. ¹⁶ And the LORD God commanded the man, saying, "Of every tree*

of the garden you may freely eat; [17] *but of the tree of the knowledge of good and evil you shall not eat, for in the day that you eat of it you shall surely die."*

Isn't prayer a good thing? Isn't belief in God a good thing? Isn't self-control a good thing? Isn't doing "good" to your fellow man a good thing? Doesn't it seem right to honor parents or other ancestors? Can it be bad to attend a place of worship? Shouldn't we respect our elders? Is it wrong to be devoted to one's belief system? Is it wrong to follow the traditions of our fathers? Everything that we do in the name of *religion* can separate us from a true relationship with God, and may not only be wrong, but also spiritually fatal. Satan is a master of using ALL of the tools available to hinder our walk with God, even "good." It seems to be a good strategy to dislodge us from God, and to fill the world with religion.

Satan's first attempt to expand his domain.

Genesis 3:1 "Now the serpent was more cunning than any beast of the field which the LORD God had made. And he said to the woman, "Has God indeed said, 'You shall not eat of every tree of the garden'?" [2] *And the woman said to the serpent, "We may eat the fruit of the trees of the garden;* [3] *but of the fruit of the tree which is in the midst of the garden, God has said, 'You shall not eat it, nor shall you touch it, lest you die.'"* [4] *Then the serpent said to the woman, "You will not surely die. ⁵ For God knows that in the day you eat of it your eyes will be opened, and you will be like God, knowing good and evil." ⁶ So when the woman saw that the tree was good for food, that it was pleasant to the eyes, and a tree desirable to make one wise, she took of its fruit and ate. She also gave to her husband with her, and he ate."*

Satan demonstrated some very clever subtlety. He did not suggest that God was dead, or that God was in any way impotent. He was more clever than that. He did suggest to Eve, and finally Adam, that there was something "more" that they could have. They could have knowledge. Is knowledge a bad thing? Being smart is good, right? What a dirty trick suggesting that Adam and Eve could be like God. It seemed to appeal to their sense of pride. It seems that the quest for knowledge can take people beyond truth. Perhaps it is easier to follow God if one does not try to be equal with God.

If I could ask Eve today about the result of her quest for knowledge, her response could be very interesting. I think that there are things she wishes she never knew: things like death, hunger, fear, mistrust, the power of Satan, and the like. The following poem may suggest some things that Eve would be better off not knowing.

152

Mother Eve

Holding him gently in her arms, she told her little son,
"He used to come and walk with us when day was almost done.
How sweet to feel His presence, how sweet to hear His voice,
His loving kindness and His care would make our hearts rejoice!
There were no trials or troubles then, there were no tears or sighs
It was His blessed presence there that made it Paradise!
You're too little now to grasp it – and it's oh, so hard to tell,
How we threw away those blessings, we were tempted and we fell.
But He loved us, though He sent us from that lovely place we knew.
He clothed us and He fed us – best of all He gave us you!"
"But now your father labors in rough and thorny ground,
To raise the foods that once just sprung up all around.
But though our sin was grievous, in His mercy He has said,
'The offspring of the woman shall bruise the serpent's head!'"
I can't quite understand it, and yet, could it be true
That the one who would conquer sin and death might possibly be you?
The little lad smiled up at her too sleepy now to speak
She saw the beauty of his eyes, the fair curve of his cheek.
She saw him as a handsome lad then as a man full grown
This cherub in a lambskin that her nimble hands had sewn.
She would teach his tiny feet to walk the path of righteousness.
She would teach those dimpled hands to do the things that God would bless.
Madonna-like she gazed at him resolved to do her part,
Holding the world's first murderer close to her loving heart.
Ethel Stichler

Satan is a liar.

John 8:44 "You are of your father the devil, and the desires of your father you want to do. He was a murderer from the beginning, and does not stand in the truth, because there is no truth in him. When he speaks a lie, he speaks from his own resources, for he is a liar and the father of it."

Jesus addressed the religious leaders of the day by condemning their religion as lies. He not only called it "lies" but he attributed the lies to the father of lies, Satan. Jesus was essentially telling the leaders, as well as the adherents of the religion, that Satan was the author of their religion. This may seem like a very strong accusation, but given the history of Satan and man, it stands to reason that Satan is the one who forms religion. Since "religion" is so very successful in separating us from God, it makes sense that religion is one of Satan's best tools.

Satan is a deceiver.

Revelation 12: 9 "So the great dragon was cast out, that serpent of old, called the Devil and Satan, who deceives the whole world; he was cast to the earth, and his angels were cast out with him."

Satan blinds men's minds with religion.

> *II Cor. 4:4 "whose minds the god of this age (Satan) has blinded, who do not believe, lest the light of the gospel of the glory of Christ, who is the image of God, should shine on them."*

Satan uses righteousness in his deception.

> *II Cor. 11:14 "And no wonder! For Satan himself transforms himself into an angel of light. ¹⁵ Therefore it is no great thing if his ministers also transform themselves into ministers of righteousness, whose end will be according to their works."*

Satan sows false doctrine.

> *Matt. 13:36 "Then Jesus sent the multitude away and went into the house. And His disciples came to Him, saying, "Explain to us the parable of the tares of the field." ³⁷ He answered and said to them: "He who sows the good seed is the Son of Man (Jesus). ³⁸ The field is the world, the good seeds are the sons of the kingdom, but the tares are the sons of the wicked one. ³⁹ The enemy who sowed them is the devil, the harvest is the end of the age, and the reapers are the angels."*

Satan is a counterfeit.

II Thess. 2:3-4, 8-10 "Let no one deceive you by any means; for that Day will not come unless the falling away comes first, and the man of sin is revealed, the son of perdition, ⁴ who opposes and exalts himself above all that is called God or that is worshiped, so that he sits as God in the temple of God, showing himself that he is God."

"And then the lawless one will be revealed, whom the Lord will consume with the breath of His mouth and destroy with the brightness of His coming. ⁹ The coming of the lawless one is according to the working of Satan, with all power, signs, and lying wonders, ¹⁰ and with all unrighteous deception among those who perish, because they did not receive the love of the truth, that they might be saved."

The whole world lies in Satan's lap.

I John 5:19 "We know that we are of God, and the whole world lies under the sway of the wicked one (Satan)."

Satan operates within the spirit world.

Ephesians 6:12 "For we do not wrestle against flesh and blood, but against principalities, against powers, against

156

the rulers of the darkness of this age, against spiritual
hosts of wickedness in the heavenly places."

The works of Satan (including religion) will be put down.

I John 3:8 "He who sins is of the devil, for the devil has
sinned from the beginning. For this purpose the Son of
God was manifested, that He might destroy the works of
the devil."

Is it uncomfortable for you to think that Satan is the author of
religion? Would you be even more uncomfortable to think the
Satan might be the author of Christianity? How about if you were
told that several million people have been killed in the name of
Christianity? Here is an example of some of the deaths resulting
from Christianity.

1562-1598 – French Wars of Religion – France – 4 million
1095-1291 – Crusades to the Holy Land – Middle East, Spain,
Africa – 1.5 million (This does include all sides of the conflict)
1184-c. 1860 – Various Christian Inquisitions – Europe – 17,500

Even though these numbers can be disputed, it is certainly true
that millions have died in the name of God, through Christianity.

Remember, there are many definitions of Christianity. I believe we would all do much better without any labels. God did not label believers, man did (or was it Satan?).

How is the Connection Made?

Jesus is the God whom we can approach without pride and before whom we can humble ourselves without despair. — *Blaise Pascal*

This is the most important question that man can ask regarding his spiritual existence. Since religion isn't the way to God, what is? Since God is reaching down to man, how does it work?

The main purpose of the entrance of Jesus into the world was to "save" people from their sins. That's why Jesus is THE Savior, THE one and only. Early in the New Testament, an angel announced to Mary and Joseph the purpose of the Messiah.

> *Matt. 1:21 "And she will bring forth a Son, and you shall call His name JESUS, for He will save His people from their sins."*

The name Jesus means "Jehovah saving." Whenever one sees the Name Jesus in the Bible, the context of the passage is centered on the idea of salvation. When one sees the Name Christ in the Bible, the context of the passage is centered on the idea of the Messiah or the promised one from the Old Testament. When one sees the name Lord in the Bible, the context has the implication of rulership, lordship, or authority. Actually, the passages can read "Lord Jesus Christ." The first word in the name is the primary context of the passage.

In the above passage, the name Jesus denotes the main focus of His coming, to save His people from their sins.

We know that salvation was purchased for man by the death of Jesus on the cross.

> *I Peter 1:23 "who, when He was reviled, did not revile in return; when He suffered, He did not threaten, but committed Himself to Him who judges righteously; ²⁴ who Himself bore our sins in His own body on the tree, that we, having died to sins, might live for righteousness—by whose stripes you were healed."*

When Jesus went to the cross, He was paying for the sins of the entire world. He bore the burden of the sin debt of the entire creation. The righteous side of God demanded death for sin, and the love side of God took the death on Himself. In the classic Messianic prophecy text from Isaiah 53, we find:

> *Isaiah 53:10 "Yet it pleased the LORD to bruise Him; He has put Him to grief. When You make His soul an offering for sin, He shall see His seed, He shall prolong His days, And the pleasure of the LORD shall prosper in His hand. ¹¹ He shall see the labor of His soul, and be satisfied.*

By His knowledge My righteous Servant shall justify many, For He shall bear their iniquities."

This passage demonstrates the overarching theme of the universe: "God is Love." The culmination of the cosmic struggle between righteousness and sin, good and evil, God and Satan, happened as Jesus went to the cross.

Since the payment for sin has been made, does that end the issue? Is it enough that God *wants* to save people? Jesus actually made a statement seemingly aimed at religious people.

> *Matt. 7:21 "Not everyone who says to Me, 'Lord, Lord,' shall enter the kingdom of heaven, but he who does the will of My Father in heaven. ²² Many will say to Me in that day, 'Lord, Lord, have we not prophesied in Your name, cast out demons in Your name, and done many wonders in Your name?' ²³ And then I will declare to them, 'I never knew you; depart from Me, you who practice lawlessness!'*

How can it be that God through Jesus is willing to die for man but still reject man? Actually He does not reject people; He rejects people who reject Him. The parable below demonstrated the displeasure of God over the very people who were entrusted with His entrance into the world, the Jews. In this passage, Jesus foretells His own rejection and ultimate death at the hands of precisely those who should have known better. They rejected Him and He, therefore, rejects them.

> *Matt. 21:33 "Hear another parable: There was a certain landowner who planted a vineyard and set a hedge around it, dug a winepress in it and built a tower. And he leased it to vinedressers and went into a far country. ³⁴ Now when vintage-time drew near, he sent his servants to the vinedressers, that they might receive its fruit. ³⁵ And the vinedressers took his servants, beat one, killed one, and stoned another. ³⁶ Again he sent other servants, more than the first, and they did likewise to them. ³⁷ Then last of all he sent his son to them, saying, 'They will respect my son.' ³⁸ But when the vinedressers saw the son, they said among themselves, 'This is the heir. Come, let us kill him and seize his inheritance.' ³⁹ So they took him and cast him out of the vineyard and killed him. "Therefore, when the owner of the vineyard comes, what will he do to those vinedressers?" ⁴¹ They said to Him, "He will destroy those wicked men miserably, and lease his vineyard to other vinedressers who will render to him the fruits in their seasons."*

Pay close attention here.

In one of the many encounters that Jesus had with the religious people of the day, one stands out as a benchmark for connecting with God. The following passages come from John chapter three. We will spend some time parsing the issues as they unfolded that evening 2,000 years ago.

John 3

> *"1 There was a man of the Pharisees named Nicodemus, a ruler of the Jews."*

First, we must find the context of this encounter. Nicodemus was a very religious man. We know that he was a Pharisee, which was one of the mainline Jewish denominations of the day. He was so well thought of in his religion that he was promoted, a "ruler" of the Jews. Note that his God was the God of Israel, the one true God. His religious heritage was no cult, it was for real. His book was the right Book, the Bible. His ancestry was that of the people chosen by God to carry the message of salvation to the entire world, the Jews. Nicodemus had enough background information to have already made the same spiritual connection with God that Mary and Joseph, Zacharias, Elizabeth, John the Baptist, Simeon and many others had already made.

> 2 *"This man came to Jesus by night and said to Him, "Rabbi, we know that You are a teacher come from God; for no one can do these signs that You do unless God is with him."*

It is interesting that Nicodemus did not ask any questions of Jesus; rather, He only made an observation that Jesus was surely from God. It does not mean that Nicodemus did not have a question, only that he did not *ask* it. From the response of Jesus, it can be implied that Nicodemus did, indeed, have a question. It's just like Jesus to not only answer a question, but also answer the heart issue that provoked the question. The response of Jesus seems to be the answer to Nicodemus' issue. After years of pondering, I feel strongly that I know the heart question that Nicodemus had: "Did I get it right?" I think that his burning issue, after all of the religion that he had practiced was, "Am I OK with God?"

> [3] *Jesus answered and said to him, "Most assuredly, I say to you, unless one is born again, he cannot see the kingdom of God."*

Now we have it! The issue is on the table for consideration. God requires a new birth for one to reach God. Regardless of what that may mean, Jesus has laid down a glaring requirement for entering Heaven, the kingdom of God. Today, one can often hear the use of the term, born again. It is often used in the form of a disclaimer, "I am a Christian, but I'm not born again." Unfortunately, that can be a very true statement as we view Christianity as a religion. The spiritual birth cannot, however, be ignored.

⁴ Nicodemus said to Him, "How can a man be born when he is old? Can he enter a second time into his mother's womb and be born?" ⁵ Jesus answered, "Most assuredly, I say to you, unless one is born of water and the Spirit, he cannot enter the kingdom of God. ⁶ That which is born of the flesh is flesh, and that which is born of the Spirit is spirit. ⁷ Do not marvel that I said to you, 'You must be born again." ⁸ The wind blows where it wishes, and you hear the sound of it, but cannot tell where it comes from and where it goes. So is everyone who is born of the Spirit."

For sure, Nicodemus did not understand that a spiritual matter was being discussed. He thought that it was physical. Jesus made the distinction clear that there is a difference between a physical and spiritual birth. The main question for me is how does a spiritual birth take place? Where would one go to experience a spiritual birth? What does a spiritual birth look like? Can I just have one?

The spiritual birth must come from a spiritual being, God. One cannot decide that he will have a spiritual birth and simply go have one somewhere; it must come from God. A spiritual transaction must occur over which man has no power, a miracle from God. This cannot come as a result of joining a religion or by attending a meeting somewhere. It is furthermore clear that Jesus told Nicodemus directly that HE must be born again. His religious zeal had not connected him to God.

> *Nicodemus answered and said to Him, "How can these things be?"*

I guess he did! How can it be that, with the highly-religious background and ancestry of Nicodemus, he had missed the mark? It was unthinkable to Nicodemus that he had done everything that he had ever been taught by his religion, but still needed something else. He needed to be born again. YOU need to be born again. We all need to be born again, or we miss heaven, a relationship with God, the spiritual benefit that God has for us in this life, and the peace that can only come from being directed by God.

Ouch!

> *Jesus answered and said to him, "Are you the teacher of Israel, and do not know these things?"*

This must surely have been a stinging criticism to Nicodemus; i.e., essentially, "What have you been teaching?" The people of Israel had been looking to Nicodemus as a teacher to teach them the way to God, and he had failed them; the religion had failed them all. Indeed, all religion will fail to find the way to God. You cannot reach up to Him via religion; He is reaching down to you via Jesus.

[16] *"For God so loved the world that He gave His only begotten Son, that whoever believes in Him should not perish but have everlasting life."*

After describing spiritual matters and alluding to Moses from the Old Testament, Jesus spelled out the missing ingredient in the life of Nicodemus, heartfelt belief. It must have amazed Nicodemus to have spent his entire religious life "doing" and not "believing." With the concept of this colossal verse, the context of the entire universe is met; God is love. How could he possibly demonstrate it better?

What kind of belief?

Is there more than one kind of belief? Apparently!

> *Romans 10:9 "that if you confess with your mouth the Lord Jesus and believe in your heart that God has raised Him from the dead, you will be saved."*

The matter is the heart, always has been the heart, and nothing but the heart, so help me God. From the heart, man must believe in Jesus as the substitutionary payment from God for man's sin. This is not religion, it is God's plan.

> *Romans 10:13 "For "whoever calls on the name of the LORD shall be saved."*

With that simple, yet deeply-profound thought in mind, we then tell God from the heart, that we accept all that He has done for us, sending Jesus to die for our sins. We accept His great demonstration of love. Calling on the Lord is simply called prayer.

A suitable prayer for salvation would go something like this:

> *Dear Lord Jesus, I am clearly a sinner and I am sorry for my sin. The best that I know how, I accept Jesus as my Savior. I need you in my life. I need you in my heart. I need you in my family. Please come into my life. Amen.*

This is not a prayer of religion. This is receiving God's way for your salvation. It must not simply be read or recited; it must be *prayed* (from the heart).

The most dangerous question.

Years ago as a corporate chaplain, I was counseling an employee. After spending some time talking about spiritual matters and the need for salvation (not religion), he asked me a question. The question was, "Isn't it possible that somewhere on my religious journey I have already been born again?" I think that he was simply trying to avoid humbling himself, and admitting his need.

Pride is an ugly thing, and it will certainly keep you from God.

The more that I thought about the question, the more dangerous I considered it. What if the answer is yes? Would a person feel comfortable limping through life hoping that he has been born again? It seems dangerous to make this assumption, costing your eternal destiny. The real question was one of religion. Isn't it OK to trust in my religion instead of experiencing a supernatural touch from God? Not according to God!

Do not delay.

> *Isaiah 55:6 "Seek ye the Lord while he may be found, call upon Him while He is near."*

It may be that as you read this book, God is nearer to you than at any time in your life. It is a very dangerous thing to test the patience of God. Ask Jesus now, from a sincere heart, to be your savior. Trust Jesus, not religion.

So What's a Guy To Do?

Whenever the method of worship becomes more important than the Person of worship, we have already prostituted our worship. There are entire congregations who worship praise and praise worship but who have not yet learned to praise and worship God in Jesus Christ. -- Judson Cornwall

In John chapter 4, Jesus had His famous encounter with the "woman at the well." It was a cross-cultural experience as she was a woman of Samaria. The Samaritans were considered by the traditional Jews as substandard people. After the Assyrian captivity of 700 BC, Cyrus, king of Persia, sent half-breed Jews back to Israel. They were a sore spot to the "pure-bred" Jews of the day, and were considered outcasts.

> John 4: "⁵ *So He came to a city of Samaria which is called Sychar, near the plot of ground that Jacob gave to his son Joseph.* ⁶ *Now Jacob's well was there. Jesus therefore, being wearied from His journey, sat thus by the well. It was about the sixth hour.* ⁷ *A woman of Samaria came to draw water. Jesus said to her, "Give Me a drink."* ⁸ *For His disciples had gone away into the city to buy food.* ⁹ *Then the woman of Samaria said to Him, "How is it that You, being a Jew, ask a drink from me, a Samaritan woman?" For Jews have no dealings with Samaritans.*

Jesus answered and said to her, "If you knew the gift of God, and who it is who says to you, 'Give Me a drink,' you would have asked Him, and He would have given you living water." The woman said to Him, "Sir, You have nothing to draw with, and the well is deep. Where then do You get that living water? Are You greater than our father Jacob, who gave us the well, and drank from it himself, as well as his sons and his livestock?" Jesus answered and said to her, "Whoever drinks of this water will thirst again, but whoever drinks of the water that I shall give him will never thirst. But the water that I shall give him will become in him a fountain of water springing up into everlasting life." The woman said to Him, "Sir, give me this water, that I may not thirst, nor come here to draw." Jesus said to her, "Go, call your husband, and come here." The woman answered and said, "I have no husband." Jesus said to her, "You have well said, 'I have no husband,' for you have had five husbands, and the one whom you now have is not your husband; in that you spoke truly." The woman said to Him, "Sir, I perceive that You are a prophet. Our fathers worshiped on this mountain, and you Jews say that in Jerusalem is the place where one ought to worship." Jesus said to her, "Woman, believe Me, the hour is coming when you will neither on this mountain, nor in Jerusalem, worship the Father. You worship what you do not know; we know what we worship, for salvation is of the Jews. But the hour is coming, and now is, when the true worshipers will worship the Father in spirit and truth; for the Father is seeking such to worship Him. God is Spirit, and those who worship Him must worship in spirit and truth." The woman said to Him, "I know that Messiah is coming" (who is called Christ). "When He comes, He will tell us all things." Jesus said to her, "I who speak to you am He."

In this classic encounter, the basic discussion was about religion: "We worship in this mountain, you worship in that mountain. Which place is correct?" Jesus let the woman know that worship had nothing to do with places or style. In fact, His answer to the woman is a benchmark for spiritual practices. If Jesus were to name or endorse a religion, this would be the place to do it. *He did neither!* He did declare the fact that salvation had been entrusted to the Jews to be spread throughout the world. It was not about being a Jew; rather, it was about believing in the God who chose them.

Pay attention here!

Jesus told the woman that those who "worship" God must worship Him in "spirit" and in "truth."

Three words are important here: worship, spirit, truth.

First, let's discuss the word worship. When one does a word study in Scripture on the word worship, several things stand out.

1. Worship is usually a physical position that demonstrates a heart attitude.

When one worships, he consciously exalts another over himself. In eastern cultures, a person will bow his head in humility as he greets another. It is a sign of honor. When a person lowers himself physically it automatically puts the other person in a higher position them himself. At the spiritual level, one exalts God by lowering himself in his own heart by bowing or experiencing personal humility.

2. Words can also be worship.

A person can worship or exalt another by the words they say. When a person brags on another or praises another, he is worshiping. Worship is a rather common thing in America as many people admire others because of their wealth or fame.

At the highest level, worship exalts God above self, material, and even that which we love the most: family.

The very first mention of worship in the Bible was when Abraham would have physically offered his son, Isaac, as a sacrifice in obedience to God.

Genesis 22: "*1 Now it came to pass after these things that God tested Abraham, and said to him, "Abraham!" And he said, "Here I am." ₂ Then He said, "Take now your son, your only son Isaac, whom you love, and go to the land of Moriah, and offer him there as a burnt offering on one of the mountains of which I shall tell you." ₃ So Abraham rose early in the morning and saddled his donkey, and took two of his young men with him, and Isaac his son; and he split the wood for the burnt offering, and arose and went to the place of which God had told him. ₄ Then on the third day Abraham lifted his eyes and saw the place afar off. ₅ And Abraham said to his young men, "Stay here with the donkey; the lad and I will go yonder and worship, and we will come back to you."*

Obviously God was testing Abraham in this story. The test was: did Abraham hold anything more dearly to his heart than God? Isaac was his only son, and a miracle son at that. Isaac was born after Abraham and his wife, Sarah, were beyond child-bearing age. Abraham was willing to put his son on a sacrificial altar and slay him in obedience to God. Abraham called this "worship." I should think so! He was willing to put God in a position that was higher than anything else in his heart, even his son. *That is worship!* Ultimately God did not require the death of Isaac. It was only a test.

Second, we have the word "spirit." In the previous chapter of this book, we talked about one becoming "born again." This is the term that Jesus used to describe the event of one becoming spiritually alive. If a person is to truly "worship" God, he must be alive spiritually. All else is a religious demonstration, and does not connect with God.

As we approach God on the spiritual level, physical demonstrations are minimized. Going to a building on Sunday does not denote worship. It's something that happens in the heart. It *could* be done in a building on Sunday, but not necessarily. Worship also does not need to take on a *form*. There are no holy *places*. There are no holy *cities*. There are no holy *garments*. There are no holy *rituals or traditions*. There are no holy *times* or *seasons* or *holidays* or *days*. There are no holy *items or relics*. And there are certainly no holy *people* perceived to be revered above all others. **Holy** is declared by God, not man.

Third, Jesus said to worship in "truth." Spiritual truth can only be determined by Scripture because the Bible is the final word on faith and practice. It is very common for "man" to take a grain of truth and, over time, package religion around it. At the basest level, most religions believe in God. From there is gets confusing. Some religions package the concept of God with: *All religions lead to God. *God is love and would never send anyone to hell. *It doesn't matter what you believe as long as you're sincere. *God can be found in a certain place, building, river,* *etc. *Certain people are needed to intercede with God for you. *Music plays an important part in worship. *Or music plays no part in worship.* And on it goes.

Three things should be considered in your worship.

Every person should be responsible for his own worship. Every person is to be held accountable for the way that he approaches God. Many people these days have been turned off by "organized" religion. Typically that means that they have seen too many practices that either cannot be justified with Scripture, or they have seen too many people in leadership who do not act spiritual.

First worship consideration. Is it Scriptural?

Precious little of what goes on in most churches today is Scriptural. In many cases, the things that we do in church are encouraged as a practice at the *personal level,* and we have incorporated them into our corporate worship. This could include practices such as singing, prayer, reading Scripture, receiving offerings, and making personal commitments to live better spiritual lives. We certainly have been encouraged to meet together, but the pattern of worship has not been dictated.

Our challenge is to determine if what we see going on around us in church is Scriptural.

Second worship consideration. Is it harmful?

In view of the fact that some of the traditions followed in church may not be Scriptural, are they harmful? Prayer is not harmful unless you are praying to a false god or to a mediator other than Jesus.

> *I Timothy 2:5 ", For there is one God and one Mediator between God and men, the Man Christ Jesus"*

Gaining converts is not harmful unless you are converting people to your religion and not to Jesus.

> *Matthew 23:15 "Woe to you, scribes and Pharisees, hypocrites! For you travel land and sea to win one proselyte, and when he is won, you make him twice as much a son of hell as yourselves."*

Baptism is not harmful unless one is trying to wash away sin by baptism. That would lead to a false hope and false sense of security which could be spiritually fatal.

> *I John 1:7 "But if we walk in the light as He is in the light, we have fellowship with one another, and the **blood of Jesus** Christ His Son cleanses us from all sin."*

Likewise, washing in the Ganges River isn't harmful unless you are lulled into thinking that it, in some way, helps cleanse people from their sin.

Third, what about preferences?

It occurs to me that God allows for preferences. We are all different. Some like music that is a little more contemporary. Even the old hymns that are sung in many churches today were at first considered sinful. Practices of the earliest churches included singing from the Psalms or other Scripture. At inception, old hymns told a more modern story but were considered modernistic.

Some people like louder preaching with a more bombastic style; some prefer a more scholarly approach. Some people like to get worked into an emotional high, while others prefer a more cerebral approach.

Some churches would consider it a sin not to give an "invitation" at the end of the message allowing people to respond publically; others are more private and less demonstrative in their delivery.

A distinction should be made between one's preferences and one's firm convictions that comes from Scripture. Unfortunately, many people are so accustomed to their preferences being met, and they have no tolerance for those who don't share those preferences.

Follow the pattern.

On the Day of Pentecost, the Holy Spirit descended on the disciples present. Under the powerful influence of the Holy Spirit of God, Peter preached his famous sermon which resulted in 3,000 people accepting Jesus as the Messiah. Shortly thereafter, under the influence of the power of God, the early church was born. The practices in those early days, empowered by the Spirit, must surely be Spirit-led worship and practice. That pattern should continue to be our benchmark for "church." Follow Acts chapter two to learn what "church" should be.

> ***Acts 2:41*** *"Then those who gladly received his word were baptized; and that day about three thousand souls were added to them."*

The first practice featured in this verse deals with "receiving" the Word. Under the powerful inspiration of the Holy Spirit, Peter delivered the Word from God. As obvious as it seems, many "churches" or worship events fail to advance God's Word. All of our theology and "religious" practice should find its basis in Scripture. A classic instruction to Timothy, a minister under the tutelage of the Apostle Paul, explains his responsibility to present a clear, accurate message from the Scripture.

II Timothy 2:15 "Be diligent to present yourself approved to God, a worker who does not need to be ashamed, rightly dividing the word of truth."

"Rightly dividing the word of truth" expresses Timothy's duty to keep his message within the bounds of Scripture. It is safe to say that most "religions" do not revere the Bible as God's Word. Even within the "Christian" religion, many churches and denominations use very little Scripture, if any, in their message. It is sad how much "religion" is taught at church, but not Scripture. We learn how to connect with God from the Bible; religion may not do that.

Once a person opens his heart, believing in Jesus, the next step taught in God's Word is to be baptized. Baptism is a highly charged and greatly misunderstood religious practice. Jesus told the early disciples to baptize those who become followers of Jesus.

Matthews 28: 19-20 "Go therefore and make disciples of all the nations, baptizing them in the name of the Father and of the Son and of the Holy Spirit, » teaching them to observe all things that I have commanded you; and lo, I am with you always, even to the end of the age."

Baptism is an act demonstrating that one identifies with Jesus. It is much like putting on a uniform once one has joined the military. The uniform is that which identifies the solder to the general public. Baptism is much like that. The act is a public display identifying the new believer as a follower of Jesus. Every believer should follow the instruction of Jesus in this way, showing a willingness to obey, without shame, the teachings of Jesus. As always, the act itself isn't as important as the heart.

> *Acts 2:42 "And they continued steadfastly in the apostles' doctrine and fellowship, in the breaking of bread, and in prayers."*

"Apostles' doctrine" denotes a willingness to accept mentorship. Finding a seasoned believer to help you along your spiritual journey is a must for a new believer. There is always someone further along than you are. Let them help you understand the ways of God. In Ephesians 4 we find that God has gifted certain people to help us reach spiritual maturity.

> *Ephesians 4: "₁₁ And He Himself gave some to be apostles, some prophets, some evangelists, and some pastors and teachers, ₁₂ for the equipping of the saints for the work of ministry, for the edifying of the body of Christ, ₁₃ till we all come to the unity of the faith and of the knowledge of the Son of God, to a perfect man, to the measure of the stature of the fullness of Christ; ₁₄ that we should no longer be children, tossed to and fro and carried about with every wind of doctrine, by the trickery of men, in the*

cunning craftiness of deceitful plotting, ₁₅ but, speaking the truth in love, may grow up in all things into Him who is the head—Christ— ₁₆ from whom the whole body, joined and knit together by what every joint supplies, according to the effective working by which every part does its share, causes growth of the body for the edifying of itself in love."

This passage talks about the journey and the ultimate destination, a mature, loving, caring, sharing, spiritually-organic mechanism which reaches out to others along the way. This is called a church. "Church" sounds religious, but it is not intended to follow man-made ideas; rather, instead, God-led worship.

From Acts 2:42 above, we also see included "fellowship" or gathering together, "breaking of bread," which probably means having communion, and shared "prayers."

"Fellowship" or gathering together, is something that we are instructed from Scripture to do.

Hebrews 10:24 "And let us consider one another in order to stir up love and good works, ₂₅ not forsaking the assembling of ourselves together, as is the manner of some, but exhorting one another…"

Mankind is certainly built to be a social creature. We draw help, knowledge, and encouragement from each other. This is certainly true at the spiritual level. We clearly need one another.

"Breaking of bread", or communion, is to be a part of these gatherings.

> *I Cor. 11:23 "For I received from the Lord that which I also delivered to you: that the Lord Jesus on the same night in which He was betrayed took bread; ²⁴ and when He had given thanks, He broke it and said, "Take, eat; this is My body which is broken for you; do this in remembrance of Me." ²⁵ In the same manner He also took the cup after supper, saying, "This cup is the new covenant in My blood. This do, as often as you drink it, in remembrance of Me." ²⁶ For as often as you eat this bread and drink this cup, you proclaim the Lord's death till He comes. ²⁷ Therefore whoever eats this bread or drinks this cup of the Lord in an unworthy manner will be guilty of the body and blood of the Lord. ²⁸ But let a man examine himself, and so let him eat of the bread and drink of the cup."*

This, too, is a highly-charged religious practice. The Apostle Paul, in his Spirit-led instructions, sets out the criteria for this remembrance. As we partake of the two elements, bread and juice, we are to focus our minds and hearts on the sacrifice that was made for us by Jesus. He gave himself to die a horrible death on the cross, paying for our sins. This practice, if done with Jesus in mind, helps us to be perpetually grateful for this ultimate act of love to us. Too often, "communion" is a mere ritual.

> *"A man who was completely innocent, offered himself as a sacrifice for the good of others, including his enemies, and became the ransom of the world. It was a perfect act." --Mahatma Gandhi*

"Prayers" are a powerful tool through which we invoke God's help in our lives and the lives of those around us. As a person bows his head in prayer for another, it creates a tremendous bond between followers of Jesus.

> *James 5:16 "Confess your trespasses to one another, and pray for one another, that you may be healed. The effective, fervent prayer of a righteous man avails much."*

Another feature of this spiritual bonding has to do with meeting the needs of others. This is highly spiritual and certainly relational.

> *Acts 2:45 "Now all who believed were together, and had all things in common, and sold their possessions and goods, and divided them among all, as anyone had need."*

The world would be a better place if people were routinely interested in helping others with their personal needs. This is actually a relational principle taught by Jesus.

> *Luke 6:38 "Give, and it will be given to you: good measure, pressed down, shaken together, and running over will be put into your bosom. For with the same measure that you use, it will be measured back to you."*

This principle has been coined "karma" by some, or "what goes around comes around" by others. The principle was also taught by Solomon in the Biblical Book of Ecclesiastes.

> *Ecclesiastes 11:2 "Cast your **bread** upon the waters, for you will find it after many days."*

The power of "community" can also be seen under the Acts 2 demonstration of the Holy Spirit of God.

> *Acts 2:46 "So continuing daily with one accord in the temple, and breaking bread from house to house, they ate their food with gladness and simplicity of heart"*

Unity is a powerful component in the human existence. It appears from the above text that "unity" is a God thing. A simple look at the world around us shows that unity is greatly missing. One can find pockets of unity, but at the global level there is a void.

Perhaps the greatest ingredient needed for unity is leadership. A common purpose or common way of thinking must be present, but with the human condition being one of selfishness, it is no wonder that commonality does not exist. Unity can scarcely be found within a single household. The divorce rate speaks to that truth. By following the lead of God through the Holy Spirit, unity can be achieved. People were led to share, give, pray, learn, and follow, caring for the needs of each other.

> *Philippians 2:4 "Let each of you look out not only for his own interests, but also for the interests of others."*

> *Acts 2:47 "praising God and having favor with all the people."*

Worship of God is the ultimate "thank you" for His goodness, majesty, wisdom, judgment and favor. As defined at the beginning of this chapter, worship is a human practice that shows devotion to God. It should be a large part of any gathering of believers. Most gatherings of today's "church services" include more "religion" than worship.

> *Luke 10:27 "'You shall love the LORD your God with all your heart, with all your soul, with all your strength, and with all your mind,' and 'your neighbor as yourself.'"*

This is the command of God: love God and love man. One

powerful characteristic of Jesus was the way that He interacted with those who honored Him.

>*Luke 4:22 "So all bore witness to Him, and marveled at the gracious words which proceeded out of His mouth."*

"Gracious words." What a novelty. Unfortunately, our world is filled with hateful, selfish words. What would Jesus do? Speak in such a way that people are filled with hope.

>*Acts 2:47 "And the Lord added to the church daily those who were being saved."*

A natural result of a Spirit-led congregation is that the Lord will add to the church or congregation people in whose lives He has performed the miracle of salvation as offered by the clear message of the Bible. When people have found Jesus, Who has yielded peace in their lives, a natural outreach takes place. Everyone wants to be at peace with God, themselves, and their fellow man.

The responsibility for worshipping God in spirit and truth falls to the worshiper. Every person is to be held to the Biblical standard. As one attends church, he has the burden to view the practices of the church with a critical eye. The pattern demonstrated above is the Spirit-led Biblical model from God. If you attend church today, how close is it to meeting that standard? Is it a "cloud without water?"

Some Will, Some Won't

"Rarely do we find men who willingly engage in hard, solid thinking. There is an almost universal quest for easy answers and half-baked solutions. Nothing pains some people more than having to think." --Dr. Martin Luther King, Jr

During New Testament days, as could be expected, "religion" quickly influenced the early churches of the day. "Church" was something new to the early believers. With some exceptions, most of the groups of that day had Jewish roots.

Through the influence of the Holy Spirit, the Apostle Paul was the catalyst for the spread of the message of Jesus, "the Gospel," throughout the mid-eastern countries. The Bible records his journeys beginning in Acts 13. He went on three trips in a near mid-eastern route, spanning more than a decade. Along the way, churches were established as Paul mentored small groups into becoming disciples of Jesus. Several of the places where Paul carried his message became notable as follow-up letters were written to these groups. These letters were called epistles, and were eventually included into the Bible as Books. The relevance of the message of these letters was far-reaching to other groups of that day, and even to the church of *this* day.

In some cases, the message of these epistles was positive,

commending the practices of the people. In some cases, warnings had to be issued about the errors of the practices of those groups, as well as heart issues that were pervasive at the time. It should be noted that none of these groups had religious labels. The name Christian had not even been well established; it didn't become popular until later. Today the name has lost its meaning. As with all religions, people move away from being truly spiritual if, in fact, they were *ever* spiritual.

Below is a list of New Testament churches and a description of how they fared against the influence of self-interest and "religion."

Antioch – Led by the Spirit of God.

> *Acts 13:* "*1 Now in the church that was at Antioch there were certain prophets and teachers: Barnabas, Simeon who was called Niger, Lucius of Cyrene, Manaen who had been brought up with Herod the tetrarch, and Saul. 2 As they ministered to the Lord and fasted, the Holy Spirit said, "Now separate to Me Barnabas and Saul for the work to which I have called them." 3 Then, having fasted and prayed, and laid hands on them, they sent them away. 4 So, being sent out by the Holy Spirit, they went down to Seleucia, and from there they sailed to Cyprus. 5 And*

when they arrived in Salamis, they preached the word of God in the synagogues of the Jews."

Galatia – Soon removed from the basic faith.

Galatians 1: "⁶ *I marvel that you are turning away so soon from Him who called you in the grace of Christ, to a different gospel,* ⁷ *which is not another; but there are some who trouble you and want to pervert the gospel of Christ.* ⁸ *But even if we, or an angel from heaven, preach any other gospel to you than what we have preached to you, let him be accursed.* ⁹ *As we have said before, so now I say again, if anyone preaches any other gospel to you than what you have received, let him be accursed."*

Philippi – Got it right.

Philippians 1: "³ *I thank my God upon every remembrance of you,* ⁴ *always in every prayer of mine making request for you all with joy,* ⁵ *for your fellowship in the gospel from the first day until now,* ⁶ *being confident of this very thing, that He who has begun a good work in you will complete it until the day of Jesus Christ;* ⁷ *just as it is right for me to think this of you all, because I have you in my heart, inasmuch as both in my chains and in the defense and confirmation of the gospel,*

194

you all are partakers with me of grace. ⁸ For God is my witness, how greatly I long for you all with the affection of Jesus Christ. ⁹ And this I pray, that your love may abound still more and more in knowledge and all discernment, ¹⁰ that you may approve the things that are excellent, that you may be sincere and without offense till the day of Christ, ¹¹ being filled with the fruits of righteousness which are by Jesus Christ, to the glory and praise of God."

Colossae – Mostly good but with defects.

Colossians 1: "³ We give thanks to the God and Father of our Lord Jesus Christ, praying always for you, ⁴ since we heard of your faith in Christ Jesus and of your love for all the saints; ⁵ because of the hope which is laid up for you in heaven, of which you heard before in the word of the truth of the gospel, ⁶ which has come to you, as it has also in all the world, and is bringing forth fruit, as it is also among you since the day you heard and knew the grace of God in truth; ⁷ as you also learned from Epaphras, our dear fellow servant, who is a faithful minister of Christ on your behalf, ⁸ who also declared to us your love in the Spirit." "⁸ Beware lest anyone cheat you through philosophy and empty deceit, according to the tradition of men, according to the basic principles of the world, and not according to Christ." "[18] Let no one cheat you of your reward, taking delight in false humility and worship of angels, intruding into those things which he has not[d] seen, vainly puffed up by his fleshly mind" "[21] "Do not touch, do not taste, do not handle," [22] which all concern things which perish with the using—according to the commandments and doctrines of men? [23] These things indeed have an appearance of wisdom in self-imposed religion, false humility, and neglect of the body, but are of no value against the indulgence of the flesh."

Thessalonica – A good example to others.

Thessalonians 1: "[2] We give thanks to God always for you all, making mention of you in our prayers, [3] remembering without ceasing your work of faith, labor of love, and patience of hope in our Lord Jesus Christ in the sight of our God and Father, [4] knowing, beloved brethren, your election by God. [5] For our gospel did not come to you in word only, but also in power, and in the Holy Spirit and in much assurance, as you know what kind of men we were among you for your sake. And you became followers of us and of the Lord, having received the word in much affliction, with joy of the Holy Spirit, [7] so that you became examples to all in Macedonia and Achaia who believe. [8] For from you the word of the Lord has sounded forth, not only in Macedonia and Achaia, but also in every place. Your faith toward God has gone out, so that we do not need to say anything. ⁹ For they themselves declare concerning us what manner of entry we had to you, and how you turned to God from idols to serve the living and true God, ¹⁰ and to wait for His Son from heaven, whom He raised from the dead, even Jesus who delivers us from the wrath to come."

Berea – More Biblical than Thessalonica.

Acts 17: "When they arrived, they went into the synagogue of the Jews. ¹¹ These were more fair-minded than those in Thessalonica, in that they received the word with all readiness, and searched the Scriptures daily to find out whether these things were so. ¹² Therefore many of them believed, and also not a few of the Greeks, prominent women as well as men."

Corinth – Pitifully prideful, divisive, and very worldly.

I Corinthians 1: "¹⁰ Now I plead with you, brethren, by the name of our Lord Jesus Christ, that you all speak the same thing, and that there be no divisions among you, but that you be perfectly joined together in the same mind and in the same judgment. ¹¹ For it has been declared to me concerning you, my brethren, by those of Chloe's household, that there are contentions among you."

I Corinthians 3: " ¹And I, brethren, could not speak to you as to spiritual people but as to carnal, as to babes in Christ. ² I fed you with milk and not with solid food; for until now you were not able to receive it, and even now you are still not able; ³ for you are still carnal. For where there are envy, strife, and divisions among you, are you not carnal and behaving like mere men?"

Jews clung to flawed tradition and were not above murdering Paul.

Acts 23:12 "¹² And when it was day, some of the Jews banded together and bound themselves under an oath, saying that they would neither eat nor drink till they had killed Paul. ¹³ Now there were more than forty who had formed this conspiracy. ¹⁴ They came to the chief priests and elders, and said, "We have bound ourselves under a great oath that we will eat nothing until we have killed Paul. ¹⁵ Now you, therefore, together with the council, suggest to the commander that he be brought down to you tomorrow, as though you were going to make further inquiries concerning him; but we are ready to kill him before he comes near."

What will you do?

We are certainly encouraged through Scripture to gather together into groups for edification (building one another up), love, ministry, and eagerly anticipating the return of Jesus.

> *Hebrews 10:24 "²⁴ And let us consider one another in order to stir up love and good works, ²⁵ not forsaking the assembling of ourselves together, as is the manner of some, but exhorting one another, and so much the more as you see the Day approaching."*

Find a body of believers which fits the pattern of Acts 2. Meet with them regularly. Encourage them; pray for them; help meet their needs. Worship God in Spirit and Truth. Learn Scripture. Grow in grace. Create a level of intimacy with Jesus. Pray about everything. Love everybody. Advance the Kingdom of God. Make known the love of God in your heart. Experience a heart relationship with Jesus. Increase your faith through use. Look for His return. Avoid sin. Keep sin confessed to Jesus. Yield to the leading of the Lord in your life. Lead your family to a spiritual walk with God through Jesus. Avoid the trappings of religion. Analyze your life constantly. Cling to truth. Heed the admonition of

> *Ecclesiastes 12:13 "Fear God, and keep his commandments: for this is the whole duty of man."*

www.ingramcontent.com/pod-product-compliance
Lightning Source LLC
Chambersburg PA
CBHW072002040426
42447CB00009B/1452